THE

ESSENTIAL

German Shepherd Dog

Consulting Editor

IAN DUNBAR, PH.D., MRCVS

Featuring Photographs by

RENÉE STOCKDALE

HOWELL
BOOK
HOUSE

Howell Book House
A Simon & Schuster Macmillan Company
1633 Broadway
New York, NY 10019

Macmillan Publishing books may be purchased for business or sales promotional use. For information please write: Special Markets Department, Macmillan Publishing USA, 1633 Broadway, New York, NY 10019.

The Essential German Shepherd Dog is an abridged edition of *The German Shepherd Dog: An Owner's Guide to a Happy Healthy Pet,* first published in 1995.

Library of Congress Cataloging-in-Publication Data
The essential german shepherd dog/featuring photographs by Renée Stockdale
p. cm.
1. German shepherd dog I. Howell Book House.
SF429.G37E77 1998 98-12637
636.737'6—dc21 CIP

ISBN 0-87605-346-0

Manufactured in the United States of America
10 9 8 7 6 5 4 3 2 1

Series Directors: Dominique DeVito, Donald Stevens
Series Assistant Directors: Jennifer Liberts, Amanda Pisani
Editorial Assistant: Michele Matrisciani
Photography Editor: Sarah Storey
Production Team: Stephanie Mohler, Heather Pope, Karen Teo
Book Design: Paul Costello
Front Cover Photo: Renée Stockdale
Back Cover Photo: Judith Strom

Many German Shepherd Dogs in interior photos courtesy of Yubon Kennels, Norman and Marilyn Woestman. Photos pages 76, 80 and 81 courtesy of Diana Robinson.

Getting to Know Your German Shepherd Dog

Ancestry

German Shepherd Dogs descend from herding dogs and even today are classified by the American Kennel Club as a herding breed. A few, but not many, German Shepherds herd sheep or cattle in the United States currently, although many German Shepherds still herd sheep and cattle in Europe. However, the instincts that

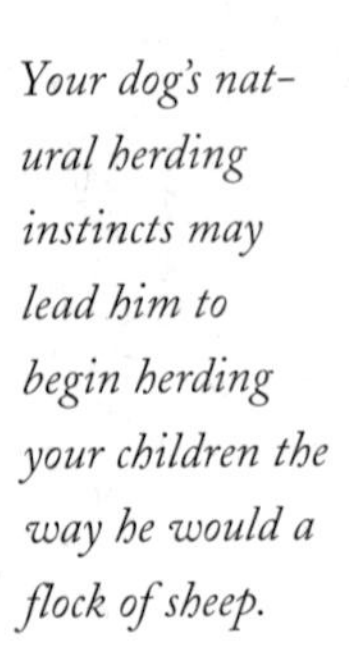

Your dog's natural herding instincts may lead him to begin herding your children the way he would a flock of sheep.

make a dog a good herding dog can still be seen in many German Shepherds, even those that have never met a sheep.

Herding dogs can show their talents in a variety of ways. One herding instinct is that of circling. With sheep or cattle, the dog would run a circle around the flock or herd to keep it in a specific area, perhaps to keep it out of a field or off the street.

Although herding instincts are very strong, they can be controlled by teaching the dog what is allowed and what isn't, and by letting the dog use his instincts constructively. Teach the dog what the real boundaries are. Many a toddler has been prevented from wandering away by an alert German Shepherd or other attentive herding dog.

Protective Instincts

The German Shepherd's instincts to guard his property come from both his herding instincts and his use as a guard dog and watchdog. When there is no flock to protect, the German Shepherd protects his people and their property. This protective instinct can be seen every day: When company approaches the house the dog will begin barking, and if a stranger approaches the family children he will start a low growl.

This protective instinct is what makes the breed so valuable to the police and military. Because of this instinct, German Shepherds do not greet every person they meet with a wagging tail and a licking tongue.

Instead, German Shepherds will stand their ground and look people in the eye. Friendly strangers may be greeted with a slightly wagging tail. Strange or threatening people will be greeted with a growl.

However, known friends will be remembered, recognized and greeted as friends.

Drive to Work

The German Shepherd was derived from herding dogs and was designed to work. This breed needs an occupation, something to keep the mind challenged and the body busy.

There are quite a few different jobs that you can give your German Shepherd. Use the dog's obedience training to give him some structure in his life and to teach him to work for you, to listen to your commands. Teach him to find your kids by name. Find someone in your area who gives herding lessons and enroll in a class. Let your dog use those instincts. Find a dog training club in your area and try something new, like agility, flyball or scent hurdle races. Teach your dog to play Frisbee. All of these things will keep your German Shepherd busy, focused and happy.

While German Shepherd puppies are little bundles of cuteness, keep in mind that full-grown Shepherds are large animals that need a lot of space.

Living with a German Shepherd Dog

Size

The German Shepherd is considered a medium- to large-sized dog, averaging from 60 to 100 pounds when full grown.

A German Shepherd's heart is not medium size, it's huge, and everything that this breed does, it does in a big way. When a German Shepherd loves you, he loves you completely. When a German Shepherd guides his blind owner, protects his law-enforcement partner, accepts obedience training, sleeps on his owner's sofa or even just chews on a rawhide, he does

German Shepherds have a particularly strong sense of smell; they love spending time sniffing around outside.

so totally, thoroughly and wholeheartedly.

Strength

The German Shepherd is a powerful dog. Without the proper training, he could easily jump on and knock down a child, a senior citizen or even an unprepared adult. After all, in law enforcement work, the breed is expected to be able to overpower criminals. However, with training, the dog can learn to restrain that power and use it only when required.

Senses

As with most dogs, the senses of smell and hearing are the most important senses to the German Shepherd. Sight, touch and taste are used, but not to the same extent as hearing and smell.

The German Shepherd's sense of smell is extremely acute. This wonderful sense of smell has enabled German Shepherds to serve humans in many ways. They can detect narcotics, contraband food, explosives, termites, gas leaks, water leaks and, of course, people.

German Shepherds can also hear better than we can. Their frequency range extends higher than ours and they can hear much fainter sounds. Another ability that surpasses ours is the ability to find exactly where a sound came from.

If a German Shepherd begins to bark very loudly, it is likely that the dog hears something suspect. You would be well-advised to investigate, rather than ignore, a German Shepherd's alarm.

Activity Level

The German Shepherd is a fairly high-energy dog that requires daily exercise—daily strenuous exercise. A 2- or 3-mile walk around the neighborhood would be good exercise for an older dog or a puppy, but cannot be considered adequate exercise for a healthy adult dog. A good run, a fast session of throwing the ball or a jog alongside a bicycle is more appropriate.

You'll find that when your German Shepherd has been exercised daily, he will be healthier, happier and more relaxed, and destructiveness around the house and yard will be decreased.

Hair, Hair and More Hair!

German Shepherds shed. There is no way to get around it. That wonderful, thick, weather-resistant coat does shed. If dog hair in the house bothers you, don't get a German Shepherd. German Shepherd owners all address the problem in

A Dog's Senses

Sight: Dogs can detect movement at a greater distance than we can, but they can't see as well up close. They can also see better in less light, but they can't distinguish many colors.

Sound: Dogs can hear about four times better than we can, and they can hear high-pitched sounds especially well. Their ancestors, the wolves, howled to let other wolves know where they were; our dogs do the same, but they have a wider range of vocalizations, including barks, whimpers, moans and whines.

Smell: A dog's nose is his greatest sensory organ. His sense of smell is so great he can follow a trail that's weeks old, detect odors diluted to one-millionth the concentration we'd need to notice them, even sniff out a person under water!

Taste: Dogs have fewer taste buds than we do, so they're likelier to try anything—and usually do, which is why it's especially important for their owners to monitor their food intake. Dogs are omnivores, which means they eat meat as well as vegetable matter, like grasses and weeds.

Touch: All dogs are social animals and love to be petted, groomed and played with, especially German Shepherds.

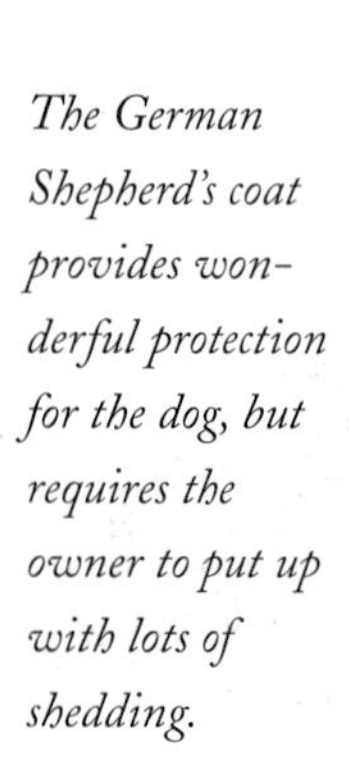

The German Shepherd's coat provides wonderful protection for the dog, but requires the owner to put up with lots of shedding.

different ways. Some vacuum daily, others buy carpet that matches the dog's coat, others pull up the carpet and put down tile. Living with a German Shepherd requires a few compromises, and understanding that the dog sheds is one of them.

The worst shedding times are spring and fall, depending upon the climate in which you live, but some shedding takes place year-round. The easiest way to keep it under control is to brush the dog thoroughly every day. Chapter 5, "Putting on the Dog" will go into more detail, but it is important to mention shedding here because it does affect how you live with your dog.

CHAPTER TWO

Homecoming

Before you bring your German Shepherd home, you will need some supplies. Some of the supplies are basic, for both the puppy and the adopted adult. Others items are specifically for one or the other.

FIRST THINGS FIRST

Food

Obviously, you will need dog food. Find out what the puppy is eating now and get some of that same food. If you wish to switch to a different brand, do so over a period of time so that your German Shepherd can adjust. Rapid changes of foods can result in problems like an upset stomach and diarrhea.

Bowls

You will need a bowl for food and a bowl for water. The food bowl can be just about anything; some people like plastic, others like ceramic or stainless steel. Whatever you use should be large enough to hold 4 to 6 cups of food and should be easy to clean. Change the water and clean the bowl daily, and if your German Shepherd likes to splash in it, check

Being prepared to bring home a new dog means having several things on hand: a crate or bed, dog food, food and water bowls, toys and grooming tools.

it several times a day to make sure the dog doesn't go thirsty.

Collar and Leash

You will also need a collar and leash for your new German Shepherd. A buckle collar, either with a metal buckle or the plastic quick-release closure, is good for both puppies and adult dogs. Adjustable collars are available that can be made larger as the puppy grows.

You will want an identification tag for your dog's buckle collar. This tag should include your name and both a daytime and an evening telephone number where you can be reached.

Crate

Your new German Shepherd will need a kennel crate to use as a bed, a place of refuge and a place for quiet time. This crate can be the plastic type that airlines require or it can be a heavy metal wire cage. The style is up to you, but the crate should be large enough for an adult German Shepherd to stand up, turn around and lie down in comfortably.

Toys

Last, but certainly not least, you will need some toys for your German Shepherd. If you are going to be bringing home a new puppy, the

toys should be something the puppy can chew on, because very shortly your puppy will start teething and will have a driving need to chew. Many dog owners like to offer rawhides (cured beef hide), while others like to give their dogs hard rubber toys to chew on. Again, it's your choice and, of course, depends on what your dog prefers. Just make sure your puppy can't chew off and swallow small pieces of the toy.

If you are bringing home an older puppy or adult German Shepherd, you will have to offer larger rawhides or indestructible toys, as German Shepherds have incredibly strong jaws. Ask at your local pet store what they have available.

Getting Your House Ready

Prior to bringing home your German Shepherd, you will need to make sure your house is ready. First of all, set up the crate in your bedroom. This way your dog will spend six to eight hours close to you and can smell and hear you all night long. This is a great way to bond with the dog, and you don't even have to do anything. Also, if the puppy needs to go outside during the night, you will hear the puppy whine and cry before there is an accident.

Next, decide where your dog will spend her days. If you are home all day, this is not a big problem; you can supervise the puppy when she's out and about. When you can't watch the pup, you can put her in her crate. However, if you work outside the home, you will need a secure place, preferably outside.

If you will be leaving your German Shepherd outside, you might want to build her a secure run or exercise area. Make sure your dog won't be able to climb or dig out of it and that other dogs, coyotes or predators can't get in. Your dog will need a house and shelter from the weather, toys and an unspillable water bowl.

Puppy Essentials

Your new puppy will need:

- food bowl
- water bowl
- collar
- leash
- ID tag
- bed
- crate
- toys
- grooming supplies

Puppy-proofing your house and providing chew toys and other proper things for her to play with are the best ways to keep your new puppy out of trouble.

Puppy-Proofing

You must make sure your house, yard and garage are safe for your new German Shepherd. It's amazing what an inquisitive puppy or bored adult dog can get into. In the house, crawl around on your hands and knees and look at things from a dog's viewpoint. Are there dangling electrical cords that might be fun to chew on? Are books or knickknacks within reach? Pick up or put away anything that looks even remotely interesting. Start teaching family members to close closet doors, pick up dirty clothes and put away shoes and slippers. With a young puppy or a new dog in the house, preventing problems from happening is imperative.

If your German Shepherd is going to have access to the garage, make sure all chemicals, paints and car parts are up high, out of reach. Many things, like antifreeze, are very poisonous. By sectioning off the garage and picking up and storing away dangerous substances, you can ensure your dog's safety.

In the yard, look for possible escape routes, places where your dog could go under or over the fence. A pile of lumber or a rabbit hutch next to the fence could provide an easy escape route.

Also in the yard, put away garden tools, fertilizers, pesticides and pool supplies. If you have potted plants, pick them up before your German Shepherd turns them into play toys. Check the list of poisonous plants (see the sidebar, "Household Dangers") to make sure your landscaping and potted plants are safe, just in case your dog does try to sample them.

SETTING UP A SCHEDULE

Dogs are creatures of habit and thrive on a regular routine that doesn't vary too much from day to day. Tiny puppies, especially, need a routine. At 8 weeks of age, puppies sleep a lot. Your puppy will eat, relieve herself, play and sleep, and a couple of hours later will repeat the whole cycle. However, as she gets older, she will gradually sleep less and play more. As she learns and develops bowel and bladder control, she will go longer periods between needing to relieve herself, from every hour to every three or four hours.

The number of "bathroom breaks" will diminish as the puppy ages. Your household routine will dictate what timetable you will set up.

Preventing Problems

Many of the commonly seen problems with dogs can be avoided through simple prevention. Puppy-proofing your house is one means of prevention.

Supervising the dog is another means of prevention. Your German Shepherd can't chew up your sofa if you supervise her while she's in the house with you. When you can't watch her, put her in her crate or outside in her pen with lots of toys. By supervising the dog, you can teach her what is allowed and what is not.

Household Dangers

Curious puppies and inquisitive dogs get into trouble not because they are bad, but simply because they want to investigate the world around them. It's our job to protect our dogs from harmful substances, like the following:

In the House

cleaners, especially pine oil

perfumes, colognes, aftershaves

medications, vitamins

office and craft supplies

electric cords

chicken or turkey bones

chocolate

some house and garden plants, like ivy, oleander and poinsettia

In the Garage

antifreeze

garden supplies, like snail and slug bait, pesticides, fertilizers, mouse and rat poisons

Quality Time with Your Dog

German Shepherds are very people-oriented dogs and must spend time with their owners. Your dog should be inside with you when you are

A crate is one of the best tools you can use to begin training your dog.

home and next to your bed at night. In addition, you will need to make time to play with your dog, train her and make sure that she gets enough exercise.

To spend time with your dog in the morning, getting up thirty minutes earlier will give you time for a fifteen- to twenty-minute walk before taking your shower. In the evening, take the children with you as you walk the dog; you can find out what's going on with the kids as you exercise your dog.

CRATE-TRAINING

Adding a puppy to your household can be a wonderful experience, but it can sour quickly if the puppy is ruining your carpets and chewing up your shoes. There is a training tool that can help—a crate.

Puppies also have a natural instinct not to soil (relieve themselves in) the place where they sleep. A crate helps housetrain a puppy by using that instinct.

Introduce the crate by opening the door and tossing a treat or toy inside. Allow the puppy to come and go as she pleases, and to investigate the crate. When she is going in and out after the treat or toy, give her a treat and close the door. Leave the door closed for a few minutes and then let the puppy out if, and only if, the puppy is being quiet. If the puppy is barking, don't let her out. If you do, you will have taught your puppy that barking works to get out.

Put the puppy in her crate when you are home and can't supervise her or when you are busy, such as eating a meal. Put the puppy in the crate when she is overstimulated—time-outs are good for puppies, too. And, of course, put the puppy in her crate for the night.

Never leave a young puppy in the crate longer than one hour, except at night when the crate is next to your bed. You may, of course, return your puppy to a crate after her "break."

CHAPTER THREE

To Good Health

The strongest body and soundest genetic background will not help a dog lead a healthy life unless he receives regular attention from his owner. Dogs are susceptible to infections, parasites and diseases for which they have no natural immunity. It is up to us to take preventative measures to make sure that none of these interferes with our dog's health. It may help to think of the upkeep of a dog's health in relation to the calendar. Certain things need to be done on a weekly, monthly and annual basis.

PREVENTIVE HEALTH CARE

Weekly grooming can be the single best monitor of a dog's overall health. The actual condition of the coat and skin and the "feel" of the body can indicate good health or potential problems. Grooming will

Run your hands regularly over your dog to feel for any injuries.

help you discover small lumps on or under the skin in the early stages before they become large enough to be seen without close examination.

You may spot fleas and ticks when brushing the coat and examining the skin. Besides harboring diseases and parasites, they can make daily life a nightmare for some dogs. Many dogs are severely allergic to even a couple of fleas on their bodies. Even if the fleas are not actually seen, their existence can be confirmed by small black specks in the coat.

Flea Control

Flea control is never a simple endeavor. Dogs bring fleas inside, where they lay eggs in the carpeting and furniture—anywhere your dog goes in the house. Consequently, real control is a matter of not only treating the dog but also the other environments the flea inhabits. The yard can be sprayed, and in the house, sprays and flea bombs can be used, but there are more choices for the dog. Flea sprays are effective for one to two weeks depending on their ingredients. Dips applied to the dog's coat following a bath have equal periods of effectiveness. The disadvantage to both of these is that some dogs may have problems with the chemicals.

Flea collars can be effective, as they prevent the fleas from traveling to your dog's head, where it's moister and more hospitable. Dog owners tend to leave flea collars on their dogs long after they've ceased to be effective. Again, some dogs may have problems with flea collars, and children should never be allowed to handle them.

Some owners opt for products that can work from the inside out. One such option is a pill (prescribed by a veterinarian) that you give to the dog on a regular basis in his food. The chemicals in the pill

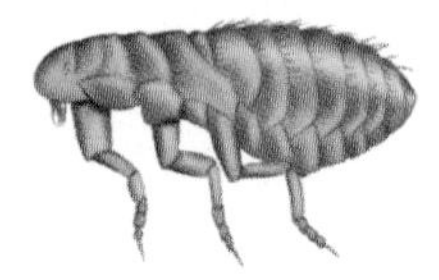

The flea is a die-hard pest.

course through the dog's bloodstream, and when a flea bites, the blood kills the flea.

Ticks

As you examine your German Shepherd, check also for ticks that may have lodged in his skin, particularly around the ears or in the hair at the base of the ear, the armpits or around the genitals. If you find a tick, which is a small insect about the size of a pencil eraser when engorged with blood, smear it thoroughly with Vaseline. As the tick suffocates in the Vaseline, it will back out and you can then grab it with tweezers and kill it. If the tick doesn't back out, grab it with tweezers and slowly pull it out, twisting very gently. Don't just grab and pull or the tick's head may separate from the body. If the head remains in the skin, an infection or abscess may result and veterinary treatment may be required.

A word of caution: Don't use your fingers or fingernails to pull out ticks. Ticks can carry a number of diseases, including Lyme disease, Rocky Mountain spotted fever and others, all of which can be very serious.

Fighting Fleas

Remember, the fleas you see on your dog are only part of the problem—the smallest part! To rid your dog and home of fleas, you need to treat your dog and your home. Here's how:

- Identify where your pet(s) sleep. These are "hot spots."
- Clean your pets' bedding, your own floors and furniture regularly by vacuuming and washing.
- Spray "hot spots" with a nontoxic, long-lasting flea larvicide.
- Treat outdoor "hot spots" with insecticide.
- Kill eggs on pets with a product containing insect growth regulators (IGRs).
- Kill fleas on pets per your veterinarian's recommendation.

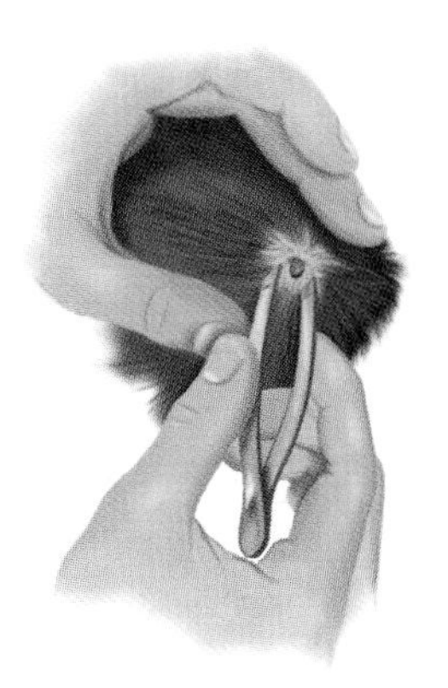

Use tweezers to remove ticks from your dog.

Proper Ear Care

Another weekly job is cleaning the ears. Many times an ear problem is evident if a dog scratches his ears or shakes his head frequently. Clean ears are less likely to develop problems, and if something does occur, it will be spotted while it can be treated easily. If a dog's ears are very dirty and seem to need cleaning on a daily basis, it is a good indication that something else is going on in the ears besides ordinary dirt and the normal accumulation of earwax. A visit to the veterinarian may indicate a situation that needs special medication.

Brushing Teeth

Regular brushing of the teeth often does not seem necessary when a dog is young and spends much of his time chewing; the teeth always seem to be immaculately clean. As a dog ages, it becomes more important to brush the teeth daily.

To help prolong the health of your dog's mouth, he should have his teeth cleaned twice a year at a veterinary clinic. Observing the mouth regularly, checking for the formation of abnormalities or broken teeth, can lead to early detection of oral cancer or infection.

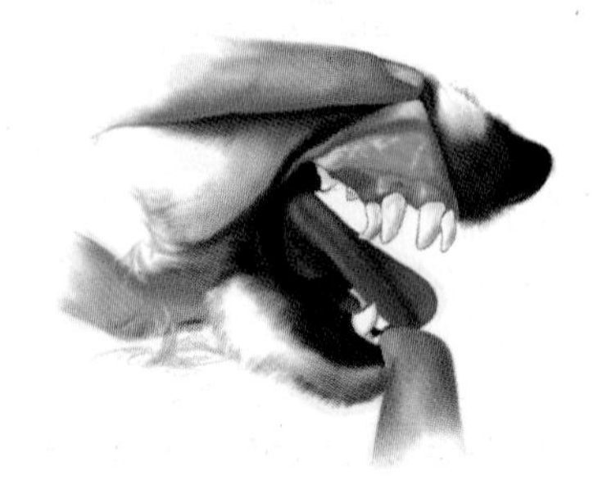

Check your dog's teeth frequently and brush them regularly.

Keeping Nails Trimmed

The nails on all feet should be kept short enough so they do not touch the ground when the dog walks.

Dogs with long nails can have difficulty walking on hard or slick surfaces. This can be especially true of older dogs. As nails grow longer, the only way the foot can compensate and retain balance is for the toes themselves to spread apart, causing the foot itself to become flattened and splayed. Over periods of time this will have a permanent effect and destroy the structure of the foot. Not only is the foot now broken down, but the legs themselves and the entire body of the dog are affected. In effect, the dog can be crippled.

Nails that are allowed to become long are also more prone to splitting. This is painful to the dog and usually requires surgical removal of the remainder of the nail for proper healing to occur. (See chapter 5 for more on nail care.)

Keeping Eyes Clear

Excessive tearing of the eyes can be an indication that a tear duct is blocked. This, too, can be corrected by a simple surgical procedure. Eye discharge that is thicker and mucous-like in consistency is often a sign of some type of eye infection or actual injury to the eye. This can be verified by a veterinarian, who will provide a topical ointment to place in the corner of the eye. Most minor eye injuries heal quickly if proper action is taken.

VACCINES

All dogs need yearly vaccinations to protect them from common deadly diseases. The DHL vaccine, which protects a dog from distemper, hepatitis and leptospirosis, is given for the first time at about 7 weeks of age, followed by one or two boosters several weeks apart. After this, a dog should be vaccinated every year throughout his life.

YOUR PUPPY'S VACCINES

Vaccines are given to prevent your dog from getting an infectious disease like canine distemper or rabies. Vaccines are the ultimate preventive medicine. That's why it is necessary for your dog to be vaccinated routinely. Puppy vaccines start at 8 weeks of age for the five-in-one DHLPP vaccine. Your veterinarian will put your puppy on a proper schedule and should remind you when to bring in your dog for shots.

Kennel cough, though rarely dangerous in a healthy dog that receives proper treatment, can be annoying. It can be picked up anywhere that large numbers of dogs congregate, such as veterinary clinics, grooming shops, boarding kennels, obedience classes and dog shows. The Bordatella vaccine, given twice a year, will protect a dog from getting most strains of kennel cough. It is often not routinely given, so it may be necessary to request it.

INTERNAL PARASITES

While the exterior part of a dog's body hosts fleas and ticks, the inside

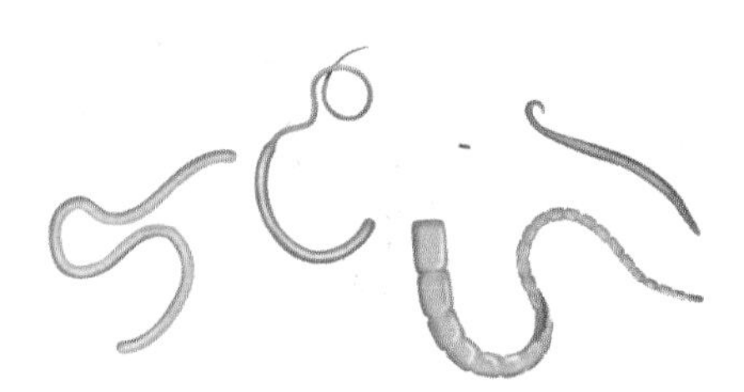

Common internal parasites (l-r): roundworm, whipworm, tapeworm and hookworm.

of the body is commonly inhabited by a variety of parasites. Most of these are in the worm family. Tapeworms, roundworms, whipworms, hookworms and heartworm all plague our dogs. There are also several types of protozoa, mainly *coccidia* and *giardia,* that cause problems.

The common tapeworm is acquired by the dog eating infected fleas or lice. Normally one is not aware that a healthy dog even has tapeworms. The only clues may be a dull coat, a loss of weight despite a good appetite or occasional gastrointestinal problems. Confirmation is by the presence of worm segments in the stool. These appear as small, pinkish-white, flattened rectangular-shaped pieces. When dry, they look like rice. If segments are not present, diagnosis can be made by the discovery of eggs when a stool sample is examined under a microscope. Ridding a dog temporarily of tapeworm is easy with a worming medicine prescribed by a veterinarian. Over-the-counter wormers are not effective for tapeworms and may be dangerous. Long-term tapeworm control is not possible unless the flea situation is also handled.

Ascarids are the most common roundworm (nematode) found in dogs. Adult dogs that have roundworms rarely exhibit any symptoms that would indicate the worm is in their body. These worms are cylindrical in shape and may be as long as 4 to 5 inches. They do pose a real danger to puppies, where they are usually passed from the mother through the uterus to the unborn puppies.

It is wise to assume that all puppies have roundworms. In heavy infestations they will actually appear in the puppy stools, though their presence is best diagnosed by a stool sample. Treatment is easy and can begin as early as 2 weeks of age and is administered every two weeks thereafter until eggs no longer appear in a stool sample or dead worms are not found in the stool following treatment. Severely infected puppies can die from roundworm infestation. Again, the worming medication should be obtained through a veterinarian.

Hookworm is usually found in warmer climates and infestation is generally from ingestion of larvae from the ground or penetration of the skin by larvae. Hookworms feed in the dog's intestine and can cause anemia, diarrhea and emaciation. As these worms are very tiny and not visible to the eye, their diagnosis must be made by a veterinarian.

Whipworms live in the large intestine and cause few if any symptoms. Dogs usually become infected when they ingest larvae in contaminated soil. Again, diagnosis and treatment should all be done by a veterinarian. One of the easiest ways to control these parasites is by picking up stools on a daily basis. This will help prevent the soil from becoming infested.

The protozoa can be trickier to diagnose and treat. Coccidiosis and giardia are the most common, and primarily affect young puppies. They are generally associated with overcrowded, unsanitary conditions and can be acquired from the mother (if she is a carrier), the premises themselves (soil) or even water, especially rural puddles and streams.

The most common symptom of protozoan infection is mucous-like blood-tinged feces. It is only with freshly collected samples that diagnosis of this condition can be made. With coccidiosis, besides diarrhea, the puppies will appear listless and lose their appetites. Puppies often harbor the protozoa and show no symptoms unless placed under stress. Consequently, many times a puppy will not become ill until he goes to his new home. Once diagnosed, treatment is quick and effective and the puppy returns to normal almost immediately.

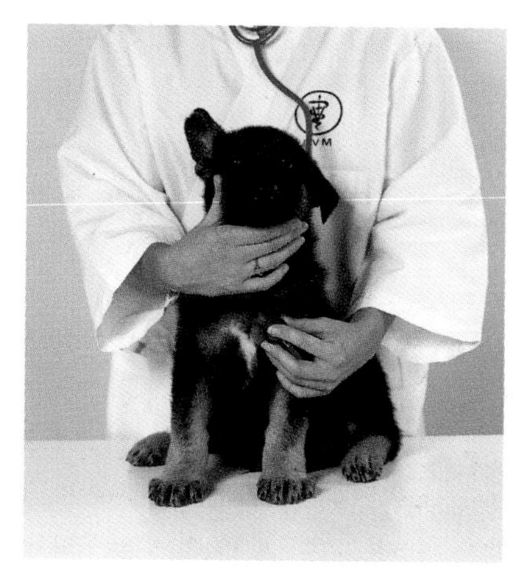

Take your German Shepherd to the vet for a checkup and to begin or continue a series of vaccinations.

Heartworm

The most serious of the common internal parasites is the heartworm. A dog that is bitten by a mosquito infected with the heartworm *microfilaria* (larvae) will develop worms

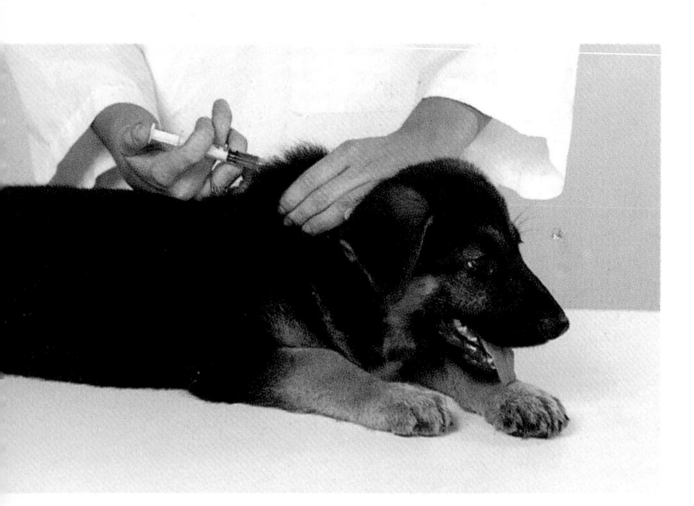

Vaccinations are an important part of your pet's health care.

that are 6 to 12 inches long. As these worms mature they take up residence in the dog's heart.

The symptoms of heartworm may include coughing, tiring easily, difficulty breathing and weight loss. Heart failure and liver disease may eventually result. Verification of heartworm infection is done by drawing blood and screening for the microfilaria.

In areas where heartworm is a risk, it is best to place a dog on a preventative, usually a pill given once a month.

At least once a year a dog should have a full veterinary examination. The overall condition of the dog can be observed and a blood sample collected for a complete yearly screening. This way the dog's thyroid functions can be tested, and the job the dog's organs are doing can be monitored. If there are any problems, this form of testing can spot trouble areas while they are easily treatable.

Proper care, regular vaccinations, periodic stool checks and preventative medications for such things as heartworm will all help ensure your dog's health.

Spaying/Neutering

Spaying a female dog or neutering a male is another way to make sure they lead long and healthy lives. Females spayed at a young age have almost no risk of developing mammary tumors or reproductive problems. Neutering a male is an excellent solution to dog aggression and also removes the chances of testicular cancer.

Female dogs usually experience their first heat cycle somewhere between 6 months and 1 year of age. Unless spayed they will continue to come into heat on a regular cycle. The length of time between heats varies, with anything from every six months to a year being normal.

There is absolutely no benefit to a female having a first season before being spayed, nor in letting her have a litter. The decision to breed any dog should never be taken lightly. The obvious considerations are whether he or she is a good physical specimen of the breed and has a sound temperament. There are several genetic problems that are common to German Shepherds, such as hip dysplasia, permeal degeneration and thyroid disease. Responsible breeders screen for these maladies prior to making breeding decisions.

Finding suitable homes for puppies is another serious consideration. Due to their popularity, many people are attracted to German Shepherds and seek puppies without realizing the drawbacks of the breed.

Owning a dog is a lifetime commitment to that animal. There are so many unwanted dogs—and yes, even unwanted German Shepherds—that people must be absolutely sure that they are not just adding to the pet overpopulation problem. When breeding a litter of puppies, it is more likely that you will lose more than you will make, when time, effort, equipment and veterinary costs are factored in.

If a male German Shepherd shows signs of aggression toward other dogs, neutering will almost always alleviate this situation.

Advantage of Spaying/Neutering

The greatest advantage of spaying (for females) or neutering (for males) your dog is that you are guaranteed that your dog will not produce puppies. There are too many puppies already available for too few homes. There are other advantages as well.

Advantages of Spaying

No messy heats.

No "suitors" howling at your windows or waiting in your yard.

Prevents pyometra (disease of the uterus) and decreases the incidence of breast cancer.

Advantages of Neutering

Decreases fights, but doesn't affect the dog's personality.

Decreases roaming.

Decreased incidences of urogenital diseases.

Should You Call the Vet?

Throughout a dog's life there are times when an owner must decide whether certain conditions require

veterinary attention. Owners should always have a good idea of what is normal for their dogs so that they have a basis for comparison when an abnormal situation is suspected.

"Normal" includes appearance, energy, eating and elimination patterns, pulse and temperature. Establish your dog's normal temperature at different times of the day to use as a guideline. Take your dog's temperature with a rectal thermometer. Be sure to shake it down to 96° and place a small amount of petroleum jelly on the tip prior to insertion. It is easiest to do this if the dog is standing. Lift up the tail and carefully insert the bulb end of the thermometer about 1½ inches into the anal opening. Don't let go, but leave it in for two to three minutes for the most accurate reading. The normal range for a healthy adult dog is 100° to 102.5°.

A dog's pulse, which is the same as his heartbeat, is taken by feeling the femoral artery, which is located in the groin region where the leg and body meet. The normal pulse is 70 to 130 beats per minute. It will vary according to the size of the dog and is faster in puppies than adults. A very athletic dog may have a slower pulse than normal. Knowing these two indicators of the dog's internal system is an invaluable aid in determining illness or infection.

Lameness

A limp that appears from nowhere and gets progressively worse is cause for concern. The first thing to do is try to ascertain where the problem actually is. Check the legs and feet for any areas of tenderness, swelling or infection. There are numerous possibilities to consider. In young, developing dogs, lameness in the rear can be an indication of hip dysplasia.

Hip dysplasia is a malformation of the ball and socket joint of the hips and can affect one or both sides of the dog. As a dog ages these joints wear down, and eventually arthritis is associated with the disease. Hip dysplasia can only be properly diagnosed by x-ray.

If x-rays do confirm hip dysplasia, there are several considerations. Surgery is one alternative in more serious cases. In very serious cases the hips themselves are removed and may be replaced with Teflon hips. Most mildly and many moderately dysplastic dogs will lead normal lives if properly managed. A dysplastic dog should be kept in good weight and physical condition. Moderate exercise, especially swimming, is necessary if a dysplastic dog is to lead a normal life. If pain develops with age, it can be relieved with aspirin.

Another serious concern with lameness, especially as a dog ages, is bone cancer. This can only be confirmed by tests and x-rays.

Not Eating or Vomiting

One of the surest signs that a German Shepherd may be ill is if he does not eat. This is why it is important to know your dog's eating habits. For most dogs one missed meal under normal conditions is not cause for alarm, but more than that and it is time to take your dog to the veterinarian to search for reasons. The vital signs should be checked and gums examined. Normally a dog's gums are pink; if ill they will be pale and gray.

There are many reasons why dogs vomit, and many of them are not cause for alarm. You should be concerned when your dog vomits frequently over the period of a day.

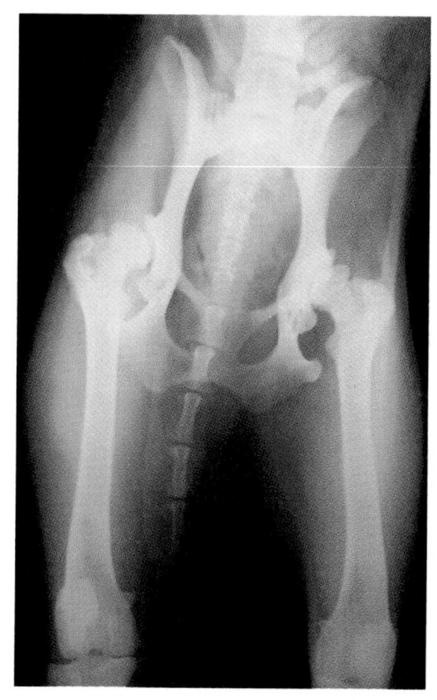

Hip dysplasia, a disease frequently seen in German Shepherds, is characterized by a failure of the head of the femur to fit properly into the hip socket.

If the vomiting is associated with diarrhea, elevated temperature and lethargy, the cause is most likely a virus. The dog should receive supportive veterinary treatment if recovery is to proceed quickly. Vomiting that is not associated with other symptoms is often an indication of an intestinal blockage. Rocks, toys and clothing will lodge in a dog's intestine, preventing the normal passage of digested foods and liquids.

If a blockage is suspected, the first thing to do is an x-ray of the stomach and intestinal region.

When to Call the Veterinarian

In any emergency situation, you should call your veterinarian immediately. You can make the difference in your dog's life by staying as calm as possible when you call and by giving the veterinarian or the assistant as much information as possible before you leave for the clinic. That way, the staff will be able to take immediate, specific action to remedy your dog's situation.

Emergencies include acute abdominal pain, suspected poisoning, snakebite, burns, frostbite, shock, dehydration, abnormal vomiting or bleeding and deep wounds. You are the best judge of your dog's health, as you live with and observe him every day. Don't hesitate to call your veterinarian if you suspect trouble.

Sometimes objects will pass on their own, but usually surgical removal of the object is necessary.

Diarrhea

Diarrhea is characterized as very loose to watery stools that a dog has difficulty controlling. It can be caused by anything as simple as changing diet, eating too much food, eating rich human food or having internal parasites.

First try to locate the source of the problem and remove it from the dog's access. Immediate relief is usually available by giving the dog an intestinal relief medication such as Kaopectate or Pepto-Bismol. Use the same amount per weight as for humans. Take the dog off his food for a day to allow the intestines to rest, then feed meals of cooked rice with bland ingredients added. Gradually add the dog's regular food back into his diet.

If diarrhea is bloody or has a more offensive odor than might be expected and is combined with vomiting and fever, it is most likely a virus and requires immediate veterinary attention. If worms are suspected as the cause, a stool sample should be examined by a veterinarian and treatment to rid the dog of the parasite should follow when the dog is back to normal. If allergies are suspected, a series of tests can be given to find the cause. This is especially likely if, after recovery and no other evidence of a cause exists, a dog returns to his former diet and the diarrhea recurs.

Bloat

Another problem associated with the gastrointestinal system is bloat, or acute gastric dilatation. It most commonly occurs in adult dogs that eat large amounts of dry kibble. Exercise or excessive amounts of water consumed immediately following a meal can trigger the condition.

A dog with bloat will appear restless and uncomfortable. He may drool and attempt to vomit. The abdominal area will appear swollen, and the area will be painful. In severe cases the stomach actually twists on itself and a condition called torsion occurs. If you suspect that your dog is suffering from bloat, run your dog to the nearest veterinary clinic immediately.

Bloat can be prevented by feeding smaller amounts of food several times per day rather than in one large meal. Soaking the food in water prior to feeding it will also help reduce the risk of bloat. Additionally, the dog should be kept from exercising until two or three hours after eating.

Seizures

Seizures vary in severity from trembling and stiffness to frenzied, rapid movements of the legs, foaming at the mouth and loss of urine and bowel movements. The latter is usually considered a grand mal seizure.

Seizures are caused by electrical activity in the brain, and there are many reasons why they may occur. Ingestion of some poisons, such as strychnine and insecticides, will cause seizures. These are generally long lasting and severe in nature. Injuries to the skull, tumors and cancers can trigger seizures.

If there appears to be no reason for the seizure it is possible the cause is congenital epilepsy. This is particularly true if a dog is under the age of 3. From the age of 5, dogs are prone to develop old age onset epilepsy, which also may have a genetic predisposition.

Never try to touch or move a dog during a seizure. If there is anything nearby that might be knocked over by their flailing legs and injure them, move it out of the way. If the seizure does not stop within five minutes, call your veterinarian.

Even after a typical seizure, your vet may suggest you bring your dog in for an examination and blood work. If a cause is not found, the best course is usually to wait and see if your dog has another seizure. If a dog only has seizures once or twice a year there is no reason to place him on preventive medication. If seizures occur on a regular basis and are of the same nature each time, the dog is considered to have epilepsy and medication should be considered.

In typical epilepsy, the dog may act restless, weird, stare and bark for some time before the actual seizure. The seizure itself lasts several minutes. A second seizure can be triggered by turning a light on or by moving the dog as he is recovering.

If seizures are infrequent and mild, an epileptic dog can lead a fairly normal life. Owners will generally begin to see a pattern in the time of day the seizures occur and their frequency, and can plan their dog's activities accordingly. Nonetheless, it is probably not a wise idea to subject a seizure-prone dog to excessive stress or exercise. The frequency and intensity of seizures often increases as time goes by, until the quality of the dog's life is questionable.

Coughing

Throughout the day most dogs will cough to get something out of their throats and it is usually ignored. If coughing persists, then it is time to look for causes.

A common cause for a dry hacking cough is kennel cough, which is contagious and usually picked up through association with other dogs. A dog with kennel cough should receive veterinary attention and be placed on antibiotics and a cough suppressant. During treatment and recovery, the dog should be kept indoors and warm as much as possible. Kennel cough, if not cared for properly, can easily turn into pneumonia in cold conditions. Infected dogs should be isolated from other dogs until they have recovered.

Chronic coughing after exercise can also be a sign of heart failure, especially in an older dog. It may also indicate a heartworm infection. If this occurs regularly, consult your veterinarian.

Most changes in the breathing pattern of a healthy dog, such as rapid inhalations or panting, are caused by exercise, stress and heat. If a dog is having problems breathing and it is also accompanied by coughing or gagging, it may be a sign that an air passage is blocked. Check for an object lodged in your dog's throat. If you can't remove it yourself, use the Heimlich maneuver. Place your dog on his side and, using both hands palms down, apply quick thrusts to the abdomen, just below the dog's last rib. If your dog won't lie down, grasp either side of the end of the rib cage and squeeze in short thrusts. Make a sharp enough movement to cause the air in the lungs to force the object out. If the cause cannot be found or removed, then professional help is needed.

Shallow breathing can be a result of an injury to the ribs or a lung problem. A wheezing noise that can be heard as a dog breathes is an indication of a serious problem. If other symptoms include a fever and lethargy, the problem may be associated with a lung disease. The symptoms may indicate treatment for an infection. An x-ray can confirm the presence of a growth or infection in the lungs.

Sometimes a dog exhibits no greater signs that something is different than increased lethargy, weight gain and even a poor coat. It may be time to consider checking the dog's thyroid levels for a possible hypothyroid condition. Low thyroid most commonly results in a poor coat and skin and eventual infertility in an intact male or female. A thyroid test will indicate what levels of the function of the thyroid are low and whether daily thyroid medication should be given.

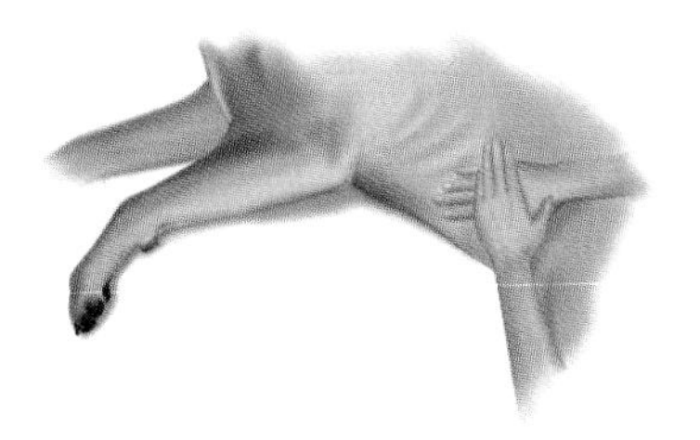

Applying abdominal thrusts can save a choking dog.

Skin Problems

Certain skin conditions should not be ignored if home treatment is not working. For example, if a dog is so sensitive and allergic to fleas that his coat and skin are literally destroyed by chewing, it is time to seek help. Cortisone can help relieve the itching and stop the dog from destroying himself, but it has side effects, too! It's best to get your vet's advice.

Mange is caused by tiny mites that live on the dog's skin. The most common types are sarcoptic and demodetic mange. Diagnosis must be made by a veterinarian, since the mites are too small to be seen.

Sarcoptic mange first occurs as small red bumps on the dog's skin and causes intense itching. If allowed to continue there is hair loss from chewing, and the affected skin becomes crusty, especially around the muzzle, elbows and hocks.

The mite that causes demodetic mange lives in the pores of the skin of most dogs. Certain conditions cause the dog's natural immunity to this mite to break down, and the result is patches of hair loss, usually around the nose or eyes. There is no itching associated with this condition and it primarily occurs in dogs under 1 year of age. If treated properly the hair returns to normal. In the generalized form of the disease, hair loss occurs in large patches all over the body. Obviously this is a much more serious condition.

Hot spots are one of the most baffling skin problems. They can be caused by a number of things, including flea bites and allergies. A warm, moist, infected area on the skin appears out of nowhere and can be several inches large. At home one should clip the hair around it, then clean it with an antiseptic and dilute (3 percent hydrogen peroxide). Spraying with a topical anaesthetic immediately relieves itching. Topical ointments can also help. If the spot is not healing and appears to be getting larger or infected, veterinary help should be sought.

A similar type of skin condition is the lick sore. These sores are almost always on the lower part of the front legs or tops of the feet. A dog will lick a spot and out of boredom continue licking it until the hair is gone and the skin is hard, red and shiny. The sore will heal on its own if kept clean and the dog is prevented access to it by an anti-chewing spray or by wearing an Elizabethan collar.

Tumors

As dogs age they are more apt to develop various types of tumors. Fatty tumors grow just under the dog's skin and are not attached to anything. These are usually benign accumulations of fatty cells. However, German Shepherds do seem prone to developing cancer, and if you see or feel any such lumps on your dog, you should consult your veterinarian. Tumors and bumps that appear and grow rapidly, are strange in color or appearance or are attached to the bone should receive immediate attention.

Cuts and Wounds

Any cut over 1/2 inch in length should be stitched for it to heal. Small cuts usually heal by themselves if they are rinsed well, washed with an antibiotic soap and checked regularly with further cleansing of soap or a hydrogen peroxide solution. When they occur in areas that are exposed to dirt, such as the feet, it may be advisable to place a wrap on the injury, but it should be removed frequently. If signs of infection appear, such as swelling, redness or warmth, it should be looked at by a veterinarian.

Puncture wounds should never be bandaged or stitched. They occur most commonly from bites, nails or wires. Anytime it is suspected that a dog might have been pierced by a nail or bitten, the body should be carefully examined for such wounds. As they often do not bleed very much they can be difficult to spot. If not treated, they can result in infection or even conditions as dangerous as tetanus.

If the wound is discovered within a short time of the occurrence, try to make it bleed by applying pressure around it. Flush it with water, then clean it with soap. Leave it exposed so that oxygen is able to stay in the wound and prevent an anaerobic condition from developing. Place a dilute hydrogen peroxide on it several times a day. Watch it carefully for any indications of infection. Anytime your dog is injured, consider placing him on an antibiotic to prevent infection.

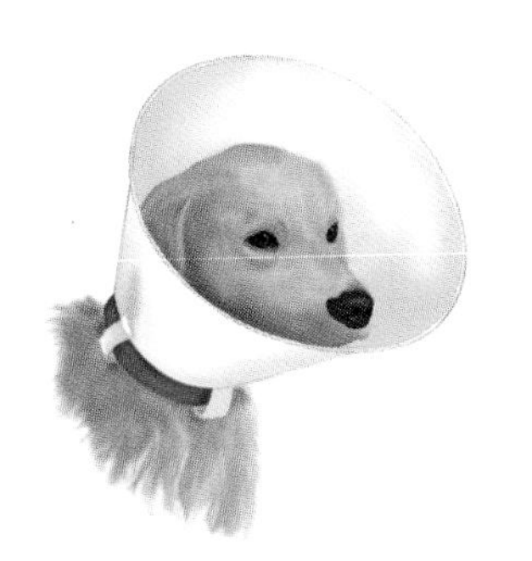

An Elizabethan collar keeps your dog from licking a fresh wound.

Giving Medication

When a dog has been diagnosed with a problem that requires medication it is usually in the form of a pill or liquid. Because it is essential for a dog to have the entire pill or capsule in order for the dosage to be effective, it's necessary to actually give the dog the pill rather than mix it in his food or wrap it in meat, which can be chewed up and spit out. Open your dog's mouth and place the pill on the back of the

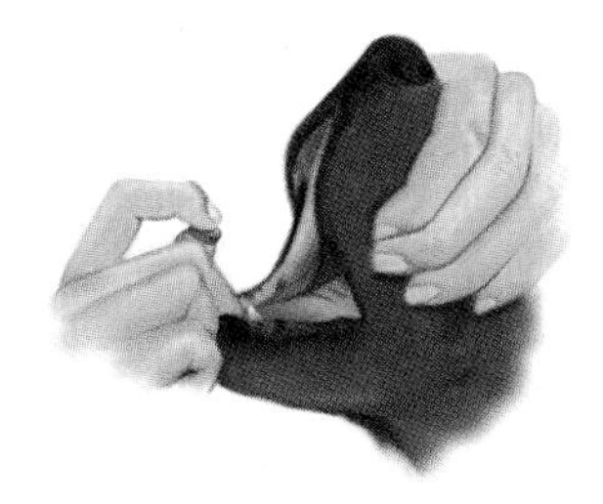

To give a pill, open the mouth wide, then drop it in the back of the throat.

middle of his tongue. Then hold his head up with his mouth held shut and stroke his throat. When the dog swallows, you can let go.

Liquid medication is most easily given in a syringe. These are usually marked so the amount is accurately measured. Hold the dog's head upward at about 45°, open the mouth slightly and place the end of the syringe in the area in the back of the mouth between the cheek and rear molars. Hold your dog's mouth shut until he swallows.

If your dog needs eye medication, apply it by pulling down the lower eyelid and placing the ointment on the inside of the lid. Then close the eye and gently disperse the solution around the eye. Eye drops can be placed directly on the eye. Giving ear medicine is similar to cleaning the ears. The drops are placed in the canal and the ear is then massaged.

Squeeze eye ointment into the lower lid.

Common German Shepherd Problems

Autoimmune Problems—The dog's immune system protects him from disease; when a virus or bacteria enters the body, white blood cells are triggered to combat the virus or bacteria. In a dog with an immune system problem, the body will not produce these white blood cells. Although the causes of autoimmune disease can vary, some researchers feel that there is a genetic predisposition toward it. Dogs with any autoimmune disease should not be used for breeding.

Bloat—Bloat was discussed earlier in this chapter. Be aware that large dogs such as German Shepherds are particularly susceptible to developing bloat and that this very serious condition requires immediate veterinary attention.

Cancer—Unfortunately, German Shepherd lineages seem to be prone to cancer. Cancer in dogs, just as in people, is not one disease but a variety of diseases. Although research is continuing, it is unknown how or why some cells go on a rampage and become cancerous.

When you examine your German Shepherd each day, be aware of any lumps or bumps you might feel, especially as your dog is growing older. Your veterinarian can biopsy any suspicious lump and if it is cancerous, many times it can be removed. Early removal has the best chance of success. Sadly, cancer is often fatal.

Hip Dysplasia—Hip dysplasia is described under the heading Lameness, earlier in this chapter. It is not uncommon in German Shepherds and dogs exhibiting lamness should be seen by a veterinarian. Any dog that is found to be dysplastic should be removed from any breeding program and spayed or neutered.

Panosteitis—Panosteitis causes lameness and pain in young, rapidly growing puppies, usually between the ages of 6 and 14 months, although it is occasionally seen in dogs up to 18 months of age. The lameness usually affects one leg at a time and can sporadically move from one leg to another. Some veterinarians prescribe pain relievers, and most suggest that the dog be kept quiet.

Identify Your Dog

It is a terrible thing to think about, but your dog could somehow, someday, get lost or stolen. How would you get him back? Your best bet would be to have some form of identification on your dog. You can choose from a collar and tags, a tattoo, a microchip or a combination of these three.

Every dog should wear a buckle collar with identification tags. They are the quickest and easiest way for a stranger to identify your dog. It's best to inscribe the tags with your name and phone number; you should not include your dog's name.

There are two ways to permanently identify your dog. The first is a tattoo, placed on the inside of your dog's thigh. The tattoo should be your social security number or your dog's AKC registration number.

The second is a microchip, a rice-sized pellet that is inserted under the dog's skin at the base of the neck, between the shoulder blades. When a scanner is passed over the dog, it will beep, notifying the person that the dog has a chip. The scanner will then show a code, identifying the dog. Microchips are becoming more and more popular and are certainly the wave of the future.

Thyroid Disease—The thyroid gland produces hormones that govern or affect a number of different bodily functions. A dog with a thyroid that is producing fewer hormones than it should may show symptoms ranging from infertility to dry, dull coat, flaky skin, runny eyes or even difficulty walking. Thyroid problems can be diagnosed with a blood test, and medication can usually relieve the symptoms fairly rapidly. In most cases, the dog will have to remain on the medication for life.

First Aid and Emergencies

While we never plan on emergencies happening, we can be partially prepared by knowing which veterinary clinics are open if something occurs at night or on the weekend. Telephone numbers should be posted so they can be easily located.

First-aid measures can be taken to help ensure that your dog gets to a veterinarian in time for treatment to be effective.

Anytime a dog is in extreme pain, even the most docile one may bite if touched. As a precaution, the dog's mouth should be restrained with some type of muzzle. A rope, pair of pantyhose or strip of cloth about 2 feet long all work in a pinch.

First tie a loose knot that has an opening large enough to easily fit around the dog's nose. Once it is on, tighten the knot on the top of the muzzle. Then bring the two ends down and tie another knot underneath the dog's chin. Finally, pull the ends behind the head and tie a knot below the ears. Don't do this if there is an injury to the head or the dog requires artificial respiration.

If a dog has been injured or is too ill to walk on his own he will have to be carried to be moved. It is important to be very careful when this is done to prevent further injury or trauma. Keep the dog's body as flat and still as possible. Two people are usually needed to move a large dog. A blanket can work if all four

Use a scarf or old hose to make a temporary muzzle, as shown.

corners are held taut. A piece of plywood or extremely stiff cardboard works best, if available.

ARTIFICIAL RESPIRATION—Artificial respiration is necessary if breathing has stopped. Situations that may cause a state of unconsciousness include drowning, choking, electric shock or even shock itself. If you've taken a course in human CPR you will discover that similar methods are used on dogs. The first thing to do is check the mouth and air passages for any object that might obstruct breathing. If you find nothing, or when it is cleared, hold the dog's mouth while covering the nose completely with your mouth. Gently exhale into the dog's nose. This should be done at between ten to twelve breaths per minute.

If the heart has stopped beating, place the dog on his right side and place the palm of your hand on the rib cage just behind the elbows. Press down six times and then wait five seconds and repeat. This should be done in conjunction with artificial respiration, so it will require two people. Artificial respiration should be continued until the dog breathes on his own or the heart beats. Heart

A First-Aid Kit

Keep a canine first-aid kit on hand for general care and emergencies. Check it periodically to make sure liquids haven't spilled or dried up, and replace medications and materials after they're used. Your kit should include:

- Activated charcoal tablets
- Adhesive tape (1 and 2 inches wide)
- Antibacterial ointment (for skin and eyes)
- Aspirin (buffered or enteric coated, not Ibuprofen or acetaminophen)
- Bandages: gauze rolls (1 and 2 inches wide) and dressing pads
- Cotton balls
- Diarrhea medicine
- Dosing syringe
- Hydrogen peroxide (3%)
- Petroleum jelly
- Rectal thermometer
- Rubber gloves
- Rubbing alcohol
- Scissors
- Tourniquet
- Towel
- Tweezers

massage should continue until the heart beats on its own or no beat is felt for five minutes.

SHOCK—Whenever a dog is injured or is seriously ill, the odds are good that he will go into a state of shock. A dog in shock will be listless, weak and cold to the touch. His gums will be pale. If not treated, a dog will die from shock, even if the illness or injuries themselves are not fatal. The conditions of the dog should continue to be treated, but the dog should be kept as comfortable as possible. A blanket can help keep the dog warm. A dog in shock needs immediate veterinary care.

SEVERE BLEEDING—When severe bleeding from a cut occurs the area should be covered with bandaging material or a clean cloth and should have pressure applied to it. If it appears that an artery is involved and the wound is on a limb, then a tourniquet should be applied. This can be made of a piece of cloth, gauze or sock if nothing else is available. It should be tied above the wound and checked every few minutes to make sure it is not so tight that circulation to the rest of the limb is cut off.

FRACTURE—If a fracture is felt or suspected, the dog should be moved and transported as carefully as possible to a veterinarian. Attempting to treat a break at home can cause more damage than leaving it alone.

POISONING—In the case of poisoning the only thing to do is get help immediately. If you know the source of the poison, take the container or object with you, as this may aid treatment.

In acidic or alkaline poisonings the chemicals must be neutralized. Pepto-Bismol or milk of magnesia at 2 teaspoons per 5 pounds of weight can be given for acids. Vinegar diluted at one part to four parts water at the same dosage can relieve alkaline poisons.

HEATSTROKE—Heatstroke occurs when a dog's body temperature greatly exceeds the normal 101.5°. It can be caused by overexercise in warm temperatures, or if a dog is left in a closed vehicle for any period of time. A dog should *never* be left in an unventilated, unshaded vehicle. Even if you only plan to be gone for a minute, that time can unexpectedly increase and place a dog in a life-threatening situation.

Dogs suffering from heatstroke will feel hot to the touch and inhale short, shallow, rapid breaths. The heartbeat will be very fast. The dog must be cooled immediately, preferably being wet down with cool water in any way that is available. The dog should be wrapped in cool, damp towels and taken to a veterinarian immediately.

The opposite of heatstroke is hypothermia. When a dog is exposed to extreme cold for long periods of time his body temperature drops, he becomes chilled and he can go into shock. The dog should be placed in a warm environment and wrapped in towels or blankets. If the dog is already wet, a warm bath can help. Massaging the body will help increase the circulation to normal levels.

Some of the many household substances harmful to your dog.

Insect Bites

The seriousness of reactions to insect bites varies. The affected area will be red, swollen and painful. In the case of bee stings the stinger should always be removed. A paste made of baking soda and water can be applied to the wound and ice applied to the area for the relief of swelling. The bites of some spiders, centipedes and scorpions can cause severe illness and lead to shock.

CHAPTER FOUR

Positively Nutritious

A healthy German Shepherd has bright, alert eyes and a shiny coat. Although good health comes from many things, including the dog's genetic heritage and her overall care and environment, good nutrition is vitally important to good health.

The Importance of Good Nutrition

The German Shepherd's body requires certain substances that she cannot manufacture herself; she must get these from the food she eats. Eventually, poor nutrition shows up as skin problems, dull, dry coat, poor stools, behavior problems, immune system deficiencies, susceptibility to disease and, eventually, a much shorter life span. A dog that is fed a balanced diet will have a shiny coat, bright eyes and lots of energy.

Commercial Dog Foods

Big Business

The major dog food companies have research departments that are constantly looking for ways to satisfy the dog owner and the dog.

There are foods for every stage of the dog's life, from puppy through senior citizen, including foods for allergic or ill dogs. All of this continuing research is aimed at providing better nutrition for dogs throughout their lives.

Quality Varies

A good quality food is necessary for your German Shepherd's health. To make sure you are using a high-quality food, read the labels on the dog-food packages (see the sidebar, "How to Read the Dog Food Label"). Make sure the food offers balanced levels of proteins, carbohydrates and fats.

Read the list of ingredients, too. If one of the first ingredients listed is "by-products," be leery of the food. Dog-food manufacturers can meet protein requirements by including by-products of inferior forms of protein.

How to Read the Dog Food Label

With so many choices on the market, how can you be sure you're feeding the right food for your dog? The information's all there on the label—if you know what you're looking for. Look for the nutritional claim right up top. Is the food "100% nutritionally complete?" If so, it's for nearly all life stages; "growth and maintenance," on the other hand, is for early development; puppy foods are marked as such, as are foods for senior dogs.

Ingredients are listed in descending order by weight. The first three or four ingredients will tell you the bulk of what the food contains. Look for the highest-quality ingredients, like meats and grains, to be among them.

The guaranteed analysis tells you what levels of protein, fat, fiber and moisture are in the food, in that order. While these numbers are meaningful, they won't tell you much about the quality of the food. Nutritional value is in the dry matter, not the moisture content.

In many ways, seeing is believing. If your dog has bright eyes, a shiny coat, a good appetite and a good energy level, chances are her diet's fine.

German Shepherds do well on a dog food that uses meat and bone meal as the first two or three ingredients. Steer away from foods with a

Types of Foods/Treats

There are three types of commercially available dog food—dry, canned and semi-moist—and a huge assortment of treats (lucky dogs!) to feed your dog. Which should you choose?

Dry and canned foods contain similar ingredients. The primary difference between them is their moisture content. The moisture is not just water. It's blood and broth, too, the very things that dogs adore. So while canned food is more palatable, dry food is more economical, convenient and effective in controlling tartar buildup. Most owners feed a 25 percent canned/75 percent dry diet to give their dogs the benefit of both. Just be sure your dog is getting the nutrition she needs (you and your veterinarian can determine this).

Semi-moist foods have the flavor dogs love and the convenience owners want. However, they tend to contain excessive amounts of artificial colors and preservatives.

Dog treats come in every size, shape and flavor imaginable, from organic cookies shaped like postmen to beefy chew sticks. Dogs seem to love them all, so enjoy the variety. Just be sure not to overindulge your dog. Factor treats into her daily caloric intake.

lot of soy or soy products, as these are thought to contribute to stomach gas, which can lead to bloat (for more on this disease, see Chapter 3, "To Good Health"). Some German Shepherds also have allergies to wheat, so you may wish to avoid wheat-based dry foods.

Feeding Your Dog

How Many Meals a Day?

Most experts recommend that puppies eat two to three times a day and adult dogs eat once or twice a day. Most dogs do very well with two meals, ten or twelve hours apart, so feed your dog after you eat breakfast and then again after you have dinner.

How Much?

Each and every German Shepherd needs a different amount of food. The dog's individual body metabolism, her activity rate and her lifestyle all affect her nutritional needs.

Most dog food manufacturers print a chart on the bag showing how much to feed your dog. It's important to note that these are suggested guidelines. If your puppy or dog is soft, round and fat, cut back on the food. If your dog is thin and always hungry, give her more food.

Individual dogs vary in how much they should eat to maintain a desired body weight—not too fat, but not too thin. Puppies need several meals a day, while older dogs may need only one. Determine how much food keeps your adult dog looking and feeling her best. Then decide how many meals you want to feed with that amount. Like us, most dogs love to eat, and offering two meals a day is more enjoyable for them. If you're worried about overfeeding, make sure you measure correctly and abstain from adding tidbits to the meals.

Whether you feed one or two meals, only leave your dog's food out for the amount of time it takes her to eat it—ten to fifteen minutes, for example. Free-feeding (when food is available any time) and leisurely meals encourage picky eating. Don't worry if your dog doesn't finish all her dinner in the allotted time. She'll learn she should.

Snacks

An occasional dog biscuit or training treat will not spoil your German Shepherd's appetite, but don't get in

To Supplement or Not to Supplement?

If you're feeding your dog a diet that's correct for her developmental stage and she's alert, healthy-looking and neither over- nor underweight, you don't need to add supplements. These include table scraps as well as vitamins and minerals. In fact, a growing puppy is in danger of developing musculoskeletal disorders by oversupplementation. If you have any concerns about the nutritional quality of the food you're feeding, discuss them with your veterinarian.

It's best to keep your dog on a regular and consistent feeding schedule.

Your puppy's nutritional needs will change as she grows, including how much and how frequently you should feed her.

the habit of offering treats. Many American dogs are overweight, and obesity is a leading killer of dogs. When you do offer treats, offer either treats made specifically for dogs or something low in calories and nutritious, like a carrot. Don't offer candy, cookies, leftover tacos or anything like that. Your German Shepherd doesn't need sugar, and chocolate is deadly for dogs. Spicy foods can cause diarrhea and an upset stomach. Play it safe and give your German Shepherd good quality, nutritious snacks very sparingly.

CHAPTER FIVE

Putting on the Dog

The German Shepherd's wonderful double coat helps make him a versatile working dog, able to function in just about any climate. This double coat, with coarse outer guard hair and a thick, softer undercoat, is also easy to keep up. It does not matt (tangle into knots), nor does it need to be trimmed.

This coat does have a drawback, though: It sheds! German Shepherds shed heavily twice a year, normally in the spring and fall, although the exact time depends upon your climate and the dog's living conditions. However, the coat sheds a little all the time, year-round.

Coat Care

If you brush your German Shepherd thoroughly two to three times a week, you can keep the hair on the floor and carpet to a minimum. There are three grooming tools you

A shedding tool is an important possession for a German Shepherd owner—you'll need to use it regularly.

should use when brushing your German Shepherd.

A pin brush looks like a woman's hairbrush. It usually has an oval head with numerous metal, pinlike bristles. This brush will go through the coat down to the skin and will loosen clumps of coat, dirt, grass seeds, burrs or other debris. Use this brush first.

To brush your dog, lie him on his side and sit or kneel next to him so that he can relax. Then, starting at his head, begin brushing in the direction the coat grows. Brush with the coat, from the head down to the tip of the tail. Then roll your dog over and do the same thing on the other side.

The next tool you will use is a shedding blade. This looks like a flexible saw blade bent into a U shape with a handle holding both blades together. This does not go through the coat but, instead, will pull out all the dead coat. With your dog still lying on his side, repeat your previous pattern, going over the dog from head to tail on each side.

You will finish by going over the dog completely with a slicker brush. This will gather all the loose coat the other brushes left behind. Follow the same pattern.

Bathing

Depending upon your German Shepherd's living environment, you may wish to bathe him once a week or once a month. If your dog is a working therapy dog, visiting nursing homes and hospitals, he will need to be bathed prior to each visit. If your dog helps herd sheep and then stays inside at night, he'll need to be bathed often. On the other hand, if your dog lives in the house with you and rarely plays outside, he may stay clean and odor free for weeks at a time. It doesn't matter how often you bathe your dog—even weekly won't hurt him, as long as you use a shampoo formulated for dogs that is gentle and conditioning.

When choosing a shampoo, ask your veterinarian or a dog groomer for recommendations; there are many shampoos on the market. When you buy the shampoo, read the label carefully. Some shampoos are to be diluted in water; others are formulated to use as is. Most shampoos formulated to kill fleas or ticks must remain on the dog for two to five minutes before being rinsed off.

You can bathe your dog outside if the weather is warm and the water from your hose isn't too cold, or you can bathe him in the bathtub. Either way, change into old clothes (you

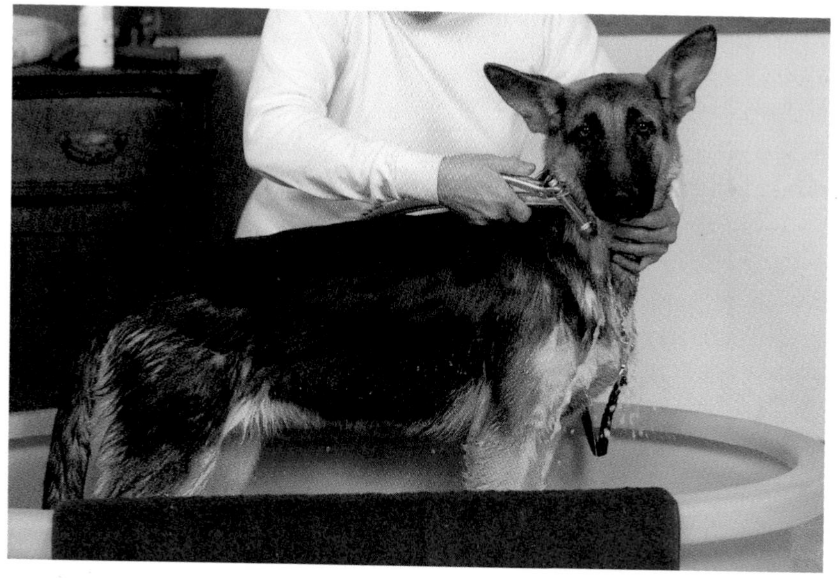

Bathing your dog may not be a fun experience for either you or your dog, but it is a necessary task to undertake at least once a month or so.

Grooming Tools

- pin brush
- slicker brush
- flea comb
- towel
- matt rake
- grooming glove
- clippers
- scissors
- nail clippers
- tooth-cleaning equipment
- shampoo
- conditioner

will get wet!) and leash your dog. Put a cotton ball in each of his ears so you don't get water in them. Make sure he is thoroughly brushed first, then use the hose or shower to get him entirely wet. It can be hard sometimes to wet the dog clear to the skin; that wonderful double coat repels water well. When wet, apply shampoo, lather and be sure to rinse *thoroughly.*

If you live in an area where fleas and ticks are prevalent and you need to dip your dog, make sure you read and follow the directions carefully. Dips are insecticides and, as such, are poisonous. Used improperly, they can cause you or your dog great harm. So be careful.

Once your German Shepherd is thoroughly rinsed, let him shake off the excess water. Dry him with a towel and, if you wish, use your blow-dryer to finish drying him. Just remember blow-dryers can get very hot, so be careful not to burn him with it.

Other Details

Ears

Each time you brush your German Shepherd, you should check his ears for dirt, wax buildup and foreign objects such as foxtails, burrs or grass seeds. Obviously, any foreign objects should be removed; if you see something you can't get, call your veterinarian immediately. If the dog's ears have a sour smell or seem to be extremely dirty, or if the dog is pawing at his ears or shaking his head, call your veterinarian immediately.

If the dog's ears are dirty or waxy, dampen a cotton ball with witch hazel and, using your finger, gently swab out the ear, getting the cotton ball into all the cracks and crevasses of the ear. You may want to use two or three cotton balls per ear.

Eyes

If your German Shepherd has some matter in the corners of his eyes, just use a damp paper towel to wipe it off; it's just like the sleep matter you sometimes have when you wake up. However, if your dog has a different type of discharge, or his eyes are red and irritated, call your veterinarian.

Teeth

If you start when your German Shepherd is a puppy, keeping his teeth clean can be easy. Take some gauze from your first-aid kit and wrap it around your index finger. Dampen it and dip it in baking soda. Take that baking soda and rub it over your dog's teeth, working gently over each tooth, the inside and the outside, and into the gum line, taking care not to hurt the dog.

Do two or three teeth and let your dog have a drink. Then work on a couple more. You may even want to break it into several sessions, doing half or a quarter of the dog's mouth at each session.

Some veterinarians recommend daily teeth cleaning. If daily cleaning is not possible, teeth should be cleaned thoroughly at least three times a week.

Nails

Your dog's toenails need to be trimmed regularly, preferably once a week. If the nails get too long, they can actually deform the foot by applying pressure against the ground, causing the toes to be in an unnatural position. Long nails are

Begin trimming your dog's toenails when he is a puppy and the task will be easier when he is fully grown.

more prone to breaking and tearing, too, and that can be as painful to the dog as it is when we tear a long fingernail. However, if the nails are trimmed regularly, you can keep them short and healthy.

Besides large-sized nail clippers, you should buy styptic powder specifically for dog nails. Keep it on hand in case you cut a nail too short. The blood vessel in a nail is referred to as the quick and serves as the blood supply to the nail. If the tip of the quick is cut, it will bleed. To be safe, only cut the hook part of the nail until you're more confident. Most of the time a minor cut to the quick will stop bleeding on its own. The stypic powder will stop the bleeding; if it doesn't, applying the powder along with some pressure does the trick. If clipping nails doesn't appeal to you, most groomers and veterinary clinics will take care of it for a small fee.

Measuring Up

What is a standard? Each breed of dog that is recognized by the American Kennel Club, or any other dog registry for that matter, has a written description called the "standard." This portrays the perfect dog of that breed, describing every aspect in detail. The standard is written by people with expert knowledge of the breed, usually a club or committee composed of longtime breeders, exhibitors and judges.

Introduction to the Standard

When a dog competes in a dog show, she is judged not only against the other dogs of her breed competing that day, but also against the

What Is a Breed Standard?

A breed standard—a detailed description of an individual breed—is meant to portray the ideal specimen of that breed. This includes ideal structure, temperament, gait and type—all aspects of the dog. Because the standard describes an ideal specimen, it isn't based on any particular dog. It is a concept against which judges compare actual dogs and breeders strive to produce dogs. At a dog show, the dog that wins is the one that comes closest, in the judge's opinion, to the standard for her breed. Breed standards are written by the breed's parent clubs, the national organizations formed to oversee the well-being of the breed. They are voted on and approved by the members of the parent clubs.

written standard. The dog that wins is the dog that most closely compares with the written description, as compared to the other dogs competing. The standard is also used to choose dogs for breeding. Breeders use the standard as a tool to see which dogs or bitches should pass on their genes to future generations.

What follow are descriptions of the ideal German Shepherd Dog. Excerpts from the breed standard appear in italics, and are followed by an explanation of their statement.

General Appearance

The first impression of a good German Shepherd Dog is that of a strong, agile, well-muscled animal, alert and full of life. It is well balanced, with harmonious development of the forequarter and hindquarter. The dog is longer than tall, deep-bodied and presents an outline of smooth curves rather than angles. It looks substantial and not spindly, giving the impression, both at rest and at motion, of muscular fitness and nimbleness without any look of clumsiness or soft living. The ideal dog is stamped with a look of quality and nobility—difficult to define, but unmistakable when present. Secondary sex characteristics are strongly marked, and every animal gives a definite impression of masculinity or femininity, according to its sex.

When judging the appearance of a German Shepherd Dog, there are three things to look for. The first relates to the dog's overall appearance: The dog should be strong, agile, well muscled and nimble. German Shepherds are meant to work, and the dog should look capable of doing so.

Next comes the dog's expression. Each dog should be aware of the world around it: alert. The word "nobility" is also used to describe the German Shepherd and is synonymous with the breed's intelligence and character, as well as its impressive physical bearing.

Third, you should look for a clear difference between the sexes. A male German Shepherd Dog should look distinctly masculine and the bitch, feminine.

Character

The breed has a distinct personality marked by a direct and fearless, but not hostile, expression, self-confidence and a certain aloofness that does not lend itself to immediate and indiscriminate friendships. The dog must be approachable, quietly standing its ground and showing confidence and willingness to meet overtures without itself making them. It is poised, but when occasion demands, eager and alert; both fit and willing to serve in its capacity as companion, watchdog, blind leader, herding dog or guardian, whichever the circumstances may demand. The dog must not be timid, shrinking behind its master or handler; it should not be nervous, looking about or upward with anxious expression or showing nervous reactions, such as tucking of tail, to strange sights or sounds. Lack of confidence

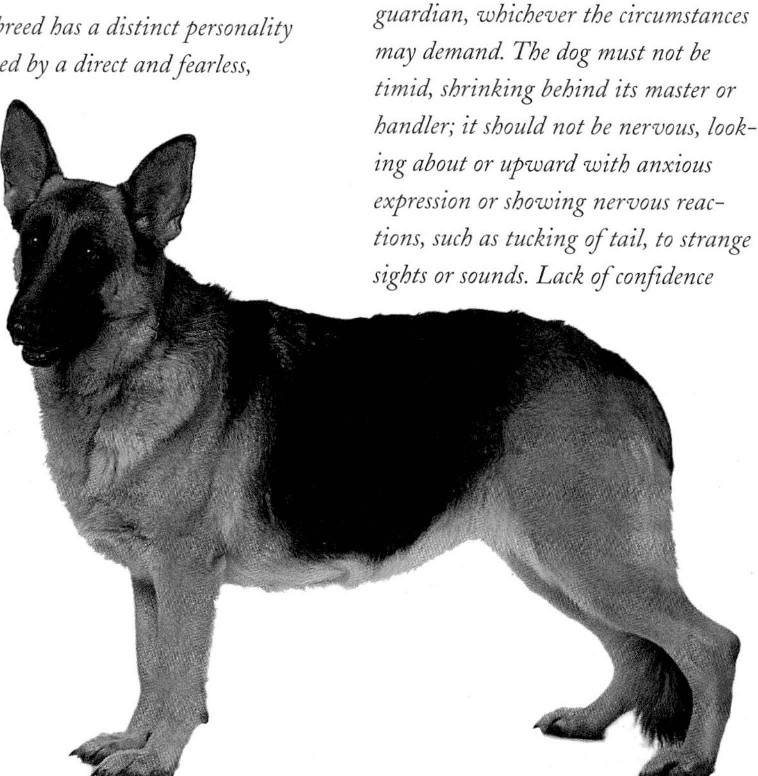

A direct, but not hostile, expression and a noble bearing are characteristic of a well-bred German Shepherd.

under any surroundings is not typical of good character.

Unfortunately, many German Shepherds do not have the correct temperament or character. Highly excitable, nervous, fearful, shy, timid or overly aggressive dogs cannot do the work the breed was designed to do. In addition, such dogs can be a danger to themselves, to their owners and to the public. A German Shepherd with correct character is a dog willing to work with its owner, a dog to be respected for its dignity and intelligence.

Head

The head is noble, cleanly chiseled, strong without coarseness, but above all not fine, and in proportion to the body. The head of the male is distinctively masculine, and that of the bitch distinctly feminine. The muzzle is long and strong with lips firmly fitted, and the topline is parallel to the topline of the skull. Seen from the front, the forehead is only moderately arched, and the skull slopes into the long, wedge-shaped muzzle without an abrupt stop. Jaws are strongly developed.

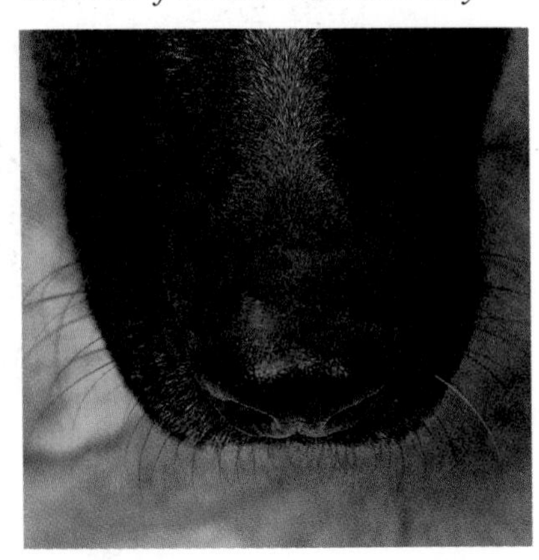

A German Shepherd's muzzle is long and wedge-shaped.

Ears

Ears are moderately pointed, in proportion to the skull, open toward the front, and carried erect when at attention, the ideal carriage being one in which the center lines ofthe ears, viewed from the front, are parallel to each other and perpendicular to the ground. A dog with cropped or hanging ears must be disqualified.

Like the head, the erect ears are another hallmark of the breed. Hanging, drooping, dropped or other incorrect ears detract from the overall appearance of the dog.

Eyes

Of medium size, almond shaped, set a little obliquely and not protruding. The color is as dark as possible. The expression is keen, intelligent and composed.

Whoever penned the adage, "The eyes are the mirror of the soul," obviously owned dogs!

Teeth

Forty-two in number—twenty upper and twenty-two lower, are strongly developed and meet in a scissors bite.

A German Shepherd's teeth can affect many areas of her daily life, from the shape of her muzzle and head, to how she eats her food, to her ability to grip a steer she needs to herd or her ability to bite a criminal she's apprehending.

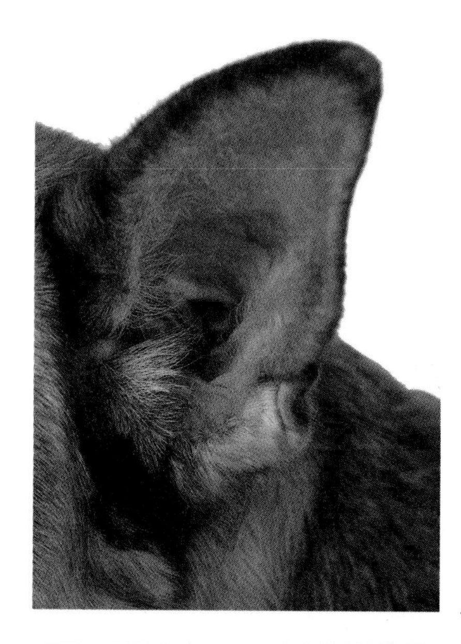

German Shepherd ears are carried erect and open to the front.

Neck

The neck is strong and muscular, clean-cut and relatively long, proportionate in size to the head and without loose folds of skin. When the dog is at attention or excited, the head is raised and the neck carried high; otherwise, typical carriage of the head is forward rather than up and only a little higher than the top of the shoulders, particularly in motion.

A long neck carrying the head somewhat forward can greatly aid a dog's movement. Long neck muscles aid the shoulders, which help forward movement. A short neck can be unattractive and can also be symptomatic of poor shoulder conformation.

An intelligent look characterizes the German Shepherd.

THE AMERICAN KENNEL CLUB

Familiarly referred to as "the AKC," the American Kennel Club is a nonprofit organization devoted to the advancement of purebred dogs. The AKC maintains a registry of recognized breeds and adopts and enforces rules for dog events including shows, obedience trials, field trials, hunting tests, lure coursing, herding, earthdog trials, agility and the Canine Good Citizen program. It is a club of clubs, established in 1884 and composed, today, of over 500 autonomous dog clubs throughout the United States. Each club is represented by a delegate; the delegates make up the legislative body of the AKC, voting on rules and electing directors. The American Kennel Club maintains the Stud Book, the record of every dog ever registered with the AKC, and publishes a variety of materials on purebred dogs, including a monthly magazine, books and numerous educational pamphlets. For more information, contact the AKC at the address listed in Chapter 9, "Further Reading and Resources."

Forequarters

The shoulder blades are long and obliquely angled, laid on flat and not placed forward. The upper arm joins the shoulder blade at about a right angle. Both the upper arm and shoulder blade are well muscled. The forelegs, viewed from all sides, are straight and the bone oval rather than round. The pasterns are strong and springy and angulated at approximately a 25-degree angle from vertical.

A dog lacking proper angulation in both the forequarters and hindquarters is less efficient while moving and is more prone to injuries. Proper angulation allows the dog to move with the effortless gait that is typical of the breed.

Feet

The feet are short, compact, with toes well arched, pads thick and firm, nails short and dark.

Solid feet with thick pads work as shock absorbers and snow tires; the feet cushion the shock of contact to the ground and they grip the ground. A dog with splayed feet, weak toes or thin pads will get footsore and be unable to work.

Proportion

The German Shepherd Dog is longer than tall, with the most desirable proportion as 10 to $8\frac{1}{2}$*. The desired height for males at the top of the highest point* *of the shoulder blade is 24 to 26 inches; for bitches, it's 22 to 24 inches. The length is measured from the point of the prosternum (or breast bone) to the rear edge of the pelvis, the ischial tuberosity.*

An easier way to visualize the proportion of the German Shepherd is to compare it to other breeds. A Basset Hound is obviously much longer than tall, as is a Dachshund. The Doberman Pinscher, on the other hand, should appear to be a square. The German Shepherd should appear to be longer than tall, but not extremely so.

A German Shepherd generally has withers that slope into the tail and a smooth, effortless gait.

Body

The whole structure of the body gives an impression of depth and solidity without bulkiness. Chest: Commencing at the prosternum, it is well filled and carried well down between the legs. It is deep and capacious, never shallow, with ample room for lungs and heart, carried well forward, with the prosternum showing ahead of the shoulder in profile. Ribs: Well sprung and long, they are neither barrel-shaped nor too flat, and are carried down to a sternum that reaches the elbows. Correct ribbing allows the elbows to move back freely when the dog is at a trot. Too round causes interference and throws the elbows out; too flat or short causes pinched elbows. Ribbing is carried well back so the loin is relatively short. Abdomen: Firmly held and not paunchy. The bottom line is only moderately tucked up in loin.

Topline

Withers: The withers are higher than and sloping into the level back. Back: The back is straight, very strongly developed without sag or roach, and relatively short. The desirable long

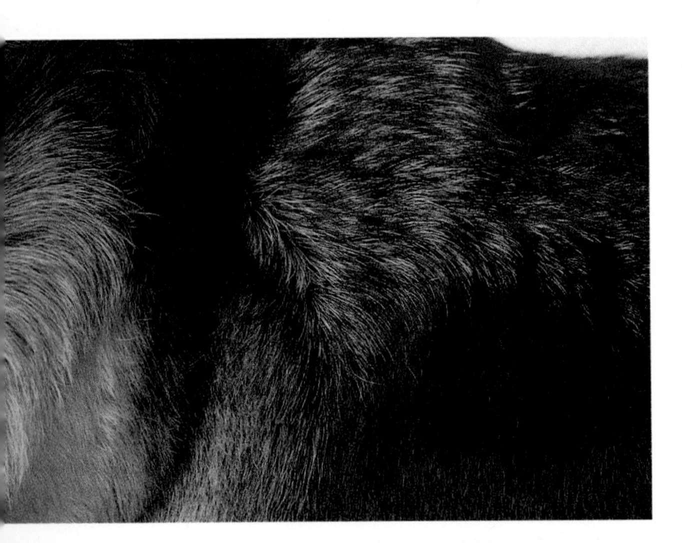

German Shepherds have a double coat: a dense, wiry outer coat and a finer, softer inner coat.

proportion is not derived from a long back but from overall length of withers and hindquarters, viewed from the side. Croup: Long and gradually sloping. Tail: Bushy, with the last vertebra extended at least to the hock joint. It is set smoothly into the croup and low rather than high.

This paragraph works together with the section describing the German Shepherd's correct proportions. The length of the shoulder blade and the length of the pelvis should be approximately the same. The pelvis should be sloped from the level back at a 30° angle. This, combined with correct shoulder angulation and sloping withers, provides for the look of a long back that the standard desires.

Hindquarters

The whole assembly of the thigh, viewed from the side, is broad, with both upper and lower thigh well muscled, forming as nearly as possible a right angle.

The hindquarter provides the power for the dog to move forward, much like a rear-wheel-driven car or a person pushing a grocery cart. Without the correct conformation, both in the hindquarters itself, but also in the back and the forequarters, power is decreased or lost.

Gait

A German Shepherd is a trotting dog, and its structure has been developed to meet the requirements of its work. General impression: The gait is outreaching, elastic, seemingly without effort, smooth and rhythmic, covering the maximum amount of ground with the minimum number of steps. At a trot the dog moves powerfully but easily, with coordination and balance, so that the gait appears to be the steady motion of a well-lubricated machine.

The trotting gait of a good German Shepherd is wonderful to watch; it's almost mystical. The dog seems to be moving without any effort at all and to be able to continue all day without fatigue.

Color

The German Shepherd varies in color, and most colors are permissible. Strong, rich colors are preferred. Nose black. Pale, washed-out colors and blues or livers are serious faults. A white dog or a dog with a nose that is not predominantly black must be disqualified.

The most commonly seen colors are black and tan, black and red, black and silver, sable and black. The black on the dog's back can range from a saddle to a complete cape. Black dogs may be entirely black or may have scattered tan, brown or gray hairs.

Although white German Shepherds have been mentioned throughout the breed's history, they are disqualified under the standard.

Coat

The ideal dog has a double coat of medium length. The outer coat should be as dense as possible, hair straight, harsh and lying close to the body. A slightly wavy outer coat, often of wiry texture, is permissible. The head, including the inner ear and foreface, and the legs and paws are covered with short hair, and the neck with longer, thicker hair. The rear of the forelegs and hindlegs has somewhat longer hair.

A Matter of Fact

Most researchers think that dogs have been a part of mankind's history for at least 12,000 years.

The first occupation of the early dogs was to guard the family's cave, warning of predators or trespassers. Dogs most certainly helped on the hunt for food and, as mankind domesticated other animals, dogs were used to protect and care for the family's livestock. Over thousands of years, herding dogs of various types were developed all over the world.

Working Dogs

In Germany, throughout history, herding dogs were selected for use by their ability to work. Dogs selected for breeding were chosen for their herding or guarding usefulness rather than their beauty. Therefore, there was no consistency of type, and certainly no one breed, used for herding.

Captain Max von Stephanitz, born in Germany in 1864, is considered the "founder" of the German Shepherd Dog.

The captain was particularly interested in the sheep herding dogs found in Germany, as they were the true working dogs of that era. These dogs varied in size, build and type but were uniformly intelligent and predisposed to work. In 1899, Captain von Stephanitz bought a working shepherd-type dog that he named Horand von Grafarth. Horand was a large dog, 24 inches tall, with good bones and clean lines. He was athletic, strong and full of life.

The First German Shepherd Dog Club

That same year, Captain von Stephanitz and his friend Artur Meyer founded the Verein für Deutsche Shäferhunde (SV), or Club for German Shepherds, and Horand became the first registered German Shepherd Dog. The club sponsored a dog show for the new breed each year beginning in 1899, and Captain von Stephanitz judged each event.

The German Shepherd's intelligence makes it a natural at obedience and agility contests.

Obedience

Since the breed's intelligence and usefulness were of utmost importance, the captain began obedience contests and herding trials. Training trials were started with awards to outstanding dogs. He also introduced the dogs to police officers, who welcomed the dogs after

Famous Owners of German Shepherd Dogs

Franklin Delano Roosevelt

Sigmund Freud

George Hamilton

Bob Hope

Jack LaLanne

Roy Rogers

finding how useful they were in apprehending criminals.

World War I introduced Captain von Stephanitz's dogs to the world. German Shepherds served as messenger dogs, worked as guard and sentry dogs and alerted their handlers to the presence of enemy soldiers. It was the breed's work with the Red Cross that earned the dogs international acclaim, however.

The Evolving German Shepherd

Around the World

The German Shepherd's working abilities spread around the world during and after World War I. European countries imported the breed in great numbers and quickly put it to work. African and South American countries, Japan and other Far East countries also imported numerous amounts.

In France, the national club is called La Société du Chien Berger Siegerschau, and sponsors an annual show in Vichy, often judged by a judge from the German SV club.

Belgium, Holland and Sweden all use working German Shepherds and import dogs from Germany as well as breed their own. Sweden has a corps of German Shepherds trained for avalanche search-and-rescue work that has been used as an example for search-and-rescue groups around the world.

Switzerland has a large number of working dogs in its police force; in fact, the ratio is one dog per every three policemen. Beginning in World War II, the German Shepherd found his niche serving as a messenger, a guard and protector, a search-and-rescue dog and a police dog.

On to the United States

American soldiers returned to the United States after World War I with tales of these wonderful dogs. Rin Tin Tin and Strongheart popularized the breed even more, and everyone wanted a German Shepherd. Unfortunately, unscrupulous breeders produced a number of unsound dogs with poor temperaments and by the late 1920s, the breed suffered a decline in popularity.

However, serious breeders continued to import good-quality dogs from Germany. Utilizing these imported dogs and carefully following Captain von Stephanitz's guidelines for breeding, breeders reestablished the German Shepherd in the United States. The first German Shepherd recognized by the American Kennel Club was Queen of Switzerland, a bitch imported from Germany. She was registered in 1908.

The breed went through another popularity surge and subsequent decline after World War II, for much the same reasons, and again serious breeders tried to bring the breed back to an even keel. They succeeded. By 1993, German Shepherds were third in popularity in American Kennel Club registrations, just behind Labrador Retrievers and Rottweilers, with over 79,000 dogs registered during the year.

Working Dog Extraordinaire

Law enforcement German Shepherds have served and continue to serve in police departments all over the United States and the world. The famous Scotland Yard police force in Britain in the 1950s kept a large corps of well-trained German Shepherds.

Law enforcement dogs search for lost people and escaping criminals, sniff for drugs or other contraband and are taught to protect their handlers and other officers at

Great intelligence and an earnest desire to work make the German Shepherd a wonderfully trainable and versatile dog.

all costs. Many courageous and loyal dogs have died serving their handlers.

The military uses dogs to search for weapons or explosives. Military German Shepherds have served on bases in the United States as well as overseas, aboard ship and in aircraft. Some have even learned to parachute, strapped to their handlers in specially designed harnesses.

Search and Rescue

The German Shepherd's strong working instincts, intelligence and wonderful scenting abilities have made it a premier search-and-rescue dog. Trained dogs and their owners have found lost hikers and campers, children who have wandered away and the elderly who might be confused and lost. German Shepherds have worked in earthquake rubble and have worked to find flood victims and people swept away by mudslides and avalanches.

Schutzhund

The sport of Schutzhund was designed to test the working abilities of German working dogs, German Shepherds in particular. Schutzhund consists of three parts: obedience, tracking and protection work. The dog must be proficient in all three areas. Schutzhund competition was founded by the German Working Dog Federation, of which the SV club is a member. In the United States, the German Shepherd Dog Club of America Working Dog Association is the primary club for German Shepherds, although several other organizations also sponsor Schutzhund trials.

Guide Dogs

Buddy, a German Shepherd bitch, was, in 1927, the first Seeing Eye dog in the United States. Today, there are several guide dog schools all over the country, and although other breeds are also used, the German Shepherd is still the breed of choice.

And More

The breed's intelligence, physical abilities and love of work have made German Shepherds useful in many different occupations. They have used their scenting abilities to find truffles, a fungus that many regard as a delicacy. Their exceptional sense of smell has enabled them to sniff out underground gas leaks in city pipes or find termites secreted in walls.

German Shepherds pull wagons, herd cattle or sheep, serve as watchdogs or guard dogs, alert the hearing disabled to sounds or dangers and much, much more. The German Shepherd is, without a doubt, a service dog *extraordinaire.*

THE ULTIMATE COMPANION DOG

Family Dogs

Although the popularity of German Shepherds began with their work with the Red Cross, Seeing Eye, the military and through Rin Tin Tin's visibility in the movies, the breed has remained popular because of its extreme loyalty toward its people. German Shepherds are devoted, responsible, loyal dogs—sometimes to a fault—and will literally give their lives for their owners.

Elizabeth Stidham, a German Shepherd breeder whose dogs compete in confomation, obedience and

WHERE DID DOGS COME FROM?

It can be argued that dogs were right there at man's side from the beginning of time. As soon as human beings began to document their existence, the dog was among their drawings and inscriptions. Dogs were not just friends, they served a purpose: There were dogs to hunt birds, pull sleds, herd sheep, burrow after rats—even sit in laps! What your dog was originally bred to do influences the way he behaves. The American Kennel Club recognizes over 140 breeds, and there are hundreds more distinct breeds around the world. To make sense of the breeds, they are grouped according to their size or function. The AKC has seven groups:

1. Sporting
2. Working
3. Herding
4. Hounds
5. Terriers
6. Toys
7. Nonsporting

Can you name a breed from each group? Here's some help: (1) Golden Retriever, (2) Doberman Pinscher, (3) Collie, (4) Beagle, (5) Scottish Terrier, (6) Maltese and (7) Dalmatian. All modern domestic dogs (*Canis familiaris*) are related, however different they look, and are all descended from *Canis lupus*, the gray wolf.

German Shepherds make loving and loyal family dogs.

tracking competitions, said, "The loyalty of the German Shepherd is legendary; the depth of its bond to its handler is well documented. Coupling courage with calm confidence, independence with compliance, derring-do with dignity, provides the balance that makes the German Shepherd Dog the world's premier working dog."

On Good Behavior

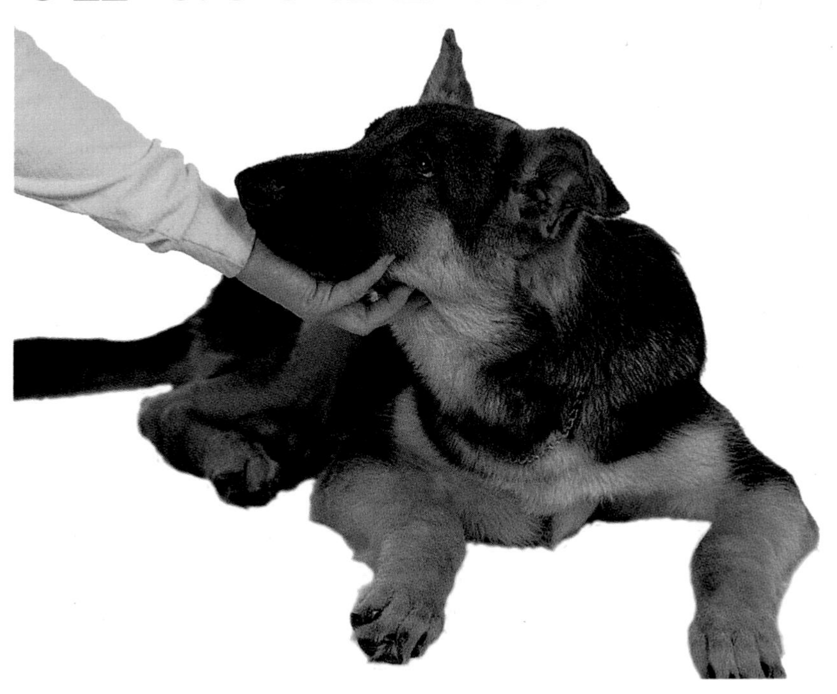

Training is the jewel in the crown—the most important aspect of doggy husbandry. There is no more important variable influencing dog behavior and temperament than the dog's education: A well-trained, well-behaved and good-natured puppydog is always a joy to live with, but an untrained and uncivilized dog can be a perpetual nightmare. Moreover, deny the dog an education and she will not have the opportunity to fulfill her own canine potential; neither will she have the ability to communicate effectively with her human companions.

Luckily, modern psychological training methods are easy, efficient, effective and, above all, considerably dog-friendly and user-friendly.

Doggy education is as simple as it is enjoyable. But before you can have a good time play-training with your new dog, you have to learn what to do and how to do it. There is no bigger variable influencing the success of dog training than the owner's experience and expertise. Before you embark on the dog's education, you must first educate yourself.

Basic Training for Owners

Ideally, basic owner training should begin well before you select your dog. Find out all you can about your chosen breed first, then master rudimentary training and handling skills. If you already have your puppydog, owner training is a dire emergency—the clock is ticking! Especially for puppies, the first few weeks at home are the most important and influential days in the dog's life. Indeed, the cause of most adolescent and adult problems may be traced back to the initial days the pup explores her new home. This is the time to establish the *status quo*—to teach the puppydog how you would like her to behave and so prevent otherwise quite predictable problems.

In addition to consulting breeders and breed books such as this one (which understandably have a positive breed bias), seek out as many pet owners with your breed as you can find. Good points are obvious. What you want to find out are the breed-specific problems, so you can nip them in the bud. In particular, you should talk to owners with adolescent dogs and make a list of all anticipated problems. Most important, test drive at least half a dozen adolescent and adult dogs of your breed yourself. An 8-week-old puppy is deceptively easy to handle, but she will acquire adult size, speed and strength in just four months, so you should learn now what to prepare for.

Puppy and pet dog training classes offer a convenient venue to locate pet owners and observe dogs in action. For a list of suitable trainers in your area, contact the Association of Pet Dog Trainers (see chapter 9). You may also begin your basic owner training by observing other owners in class. Watch as many classes and test drive as many dogs as possible. Select an upbeat, dog-friendly, people-friendly, fun-and-games, puppydog pet training class to learn the ropes. Also, watch training videos and read training books. You must find out what to do and how to do it *before* you have to do it.

PRINCIPLES OF TRAINING

Most people think training comprises teaching the dog to do things such as sit, speak and roll over, but even a 4-week-old pup knows how to do these things already. Instead, the first step in training involves teaching the dog human words for each dog behavior and activity and for each aspect of the dog's environment. That way you, the owner, can more easily participate in the dog's domestic education by directing her to perform specific actions appropriately, that is, at the right time, in the right place and so on. Training opens communication channels, enabling an educated dog to at least understand her owner's requests.

In addition to teaching a dog what we want her to do, it is also necessary to teach her why she should do what we ask. Indeed, 95 percent of training revolves around motivating the dog to want to do what we want. Dogs often understand what their owners want; they

Pet training classes are a good way to begin learning how to communicate with your dog.

just don't see the point of doing it—especially when the owner's repetitively boring and seemingly senseless instructions are totally at odds with much more pressing and exciting doggy distractions. It is not so much the dog that is being stubborn or dominant; rather, it is the owner who has failed to acknowledge the dog's needs and feelings and to approach training from the dog's point of view.

The Meaning of Instructions

The secret to successful training is learning how to use training lures to predict or prompt specific behaviors—to coax the dog to do what you want when you want. Any highly valued object (such as a treat or toy) may be used as a lure, which the dog will follow with her eyes and nose. Moving the lure in specific ways entices the dog to move her nose, head and entire body in specific ways. In fact, by learning the art of manipulating various lures, it is possible to teach the dog to assume virtually any body position and perform any action. Once you have control over the expression of the dog's behaviors and can elicit any body position or behavior at will, you can easily teach the dog to perform on request.

Tell your dog what you want her to do, use a lure to entice her to respond correctly, then profusely praise and maybe reward her once she performs the desired action. For example, verbally request "Fido, sit!" while you move a squeaky toy upwards and backwards over the dog's muzzle (lure-movement and hand signal), smile knowingly as she looks up (to follow the lure) and sits down (as a result of canine anatomical engineering), then praise her to distraction ("Gooood Fido!"). Squeak the toy, offer a training treat and give your dog and yourself a pat on the back.

Being able to elicit desired responses over and over enables the owner to reward the dog over and over. Consequently, the dog begins to think training is fun. For example, the more the dog is rewarded for sitting, the more she enjoys sitting. Eventually the dog comes to realize that, whereas most sitting is appreciated, sitting immediately upon request usually prompts especially enthusiastic praise and a slew of high-level rewards. The dog begins to sit on cue much of the time, showing that she is starting to grasp the meaning of the owner's verbal request and hand signal.

Why Comply?

Most dogs enjoy initial lure-reward training and are only too happy to comply with their owners' wishes. Unfortunately, repetitive drilling without appreciative feedback tends to diminish the dog's enthusiasm until she eventually fails to see the point of complying anymore. Moreover, as the dog approaches adolescence she becomes more easily distracted as she develops other interests. Lengthy sessions with repetitive exercises tend to bore and demotivate both parties. If it's not fun, the owner doesn't do it and neither does the dog.

Integrate training into your dog's life: The greater number of training sessions each day and the shorter they are, the more willingly compliant your dog will become. Make sure to have a short (just a few seconds) training interlude before every enjoyable canine activity. For example, ask your dog to sit to greet people, to sit before you throw her Frisbee and to sit for her supper. Really, sitting is no different from a canine "Please." Also, include numerous short training interludes during every enjoyable canine pastime, for example, when playing with the dog or when she is running in the park. In this fashion, doggy distractions may be effectively converted into rewards for training. Just as all games have rules, fun becomes training . . . and training becomes fun.

Eventually, rewards actually become unnecessary to continue motivating your dog. If trained with consideration and kindness, performing the desired behaviors will become self-rewarding and, in a sense, your dog will motivate herself. Just as it is not necessary to reward a human companion during an enjoyable walk in the park, or following a game of tennis, it is hardly necessary to reward our best friend—the dog—for walking by our side or while playing fetch. Human company during enjoyable activities is reward enough for most dogs.

Even though your dog has become self-motivating, it's still good to praise and pet her a lot and offer rewards once in a while, especially for a job well done. And if for no other reason, praising and

Many dogs respond well to lure-reward training, but will eventually grow to enjoy it enough for the interaction to be its own reward.

rewarding others is good for the human heart.

Punishment

Without a doubt, lure-reward training is by far the best way to teach: Entice your dog to do what you want and then reward her for doing so. Unfortunately, a human shortcoming is to take the good for granted and to moan and groan at the bad. Specifically, the dog's many good behaviors are ignored while the owner focuses on punishing the dog for making mistakes. In extreme cases, instruction is limited to punishing mistakes made by a trainee dog, child, employee or husband, even though it has been proven punishment training is notoriously inefficient and ineffective and is decidedly unfriendly and combative. It teaches the dog that training is a drag, almost as quickly as it teaches the dog to dislike her trainer. Why treat our best friends like our worst enemies?

Punishment training is also much more laborious and time consuming. Whereas it takes only a finite amount of time to teach a dog what to chew, for example, it takes much, much longer to punish the dog for each and every mistake. Remember, there is only one right way! So why not teach that right way from the outset?!

To make matters worse, punishment training causes severe lapses in the dog's reliability. Since it is obviously impossible to punish the dog each and every time she misbehaves, the dog quickly learns to distinguish between those times when she must comply (so as to avoid impending punishment) and those times when she need not comply, because punishment is impossible. Such times include when the dog is off leash and 6 feet away, when the owner is otherwise engaged (talking to a friend, watching television, taking a shower, tending to the baby or chatting on the telephone) or when the dog is left at home alone.

Instances of misbehavior will be numerous when the owner is away, because even when the dog complied in the owner's looming presence, she did so unwillingly. The dog was forced to act against her will, rather than molding her will to want to please. Hence, when the owner is absent, not only does the dog know she need not comply, she simply does not want to. Again, the trainee is not a stubborn vindictive beast, but rather the trainer has failed to teach. Punishment training invariably creates unpredictable Jekyll and Hyde behavior.

TRAINER'S TOOLS

Many training books extol the virtues of a vast array of training paraphernalia and electronic and metallic gizmos, most of which are designed for canine restraint, correction and punishment, rather than for actual facilitation of doggy education. In reality, most effective training tools are not found in stores; they come from within ourselves. In addition to a willing dog, all you really need is a functional human brain, gentle hands, a loving heart and a good attitude.

In terms of equipment, all dogs do require a quality buckle collar to sport dog tags and to attach the leash (for safety and to comply with local leash laws). Hollow chew toys (like Kongs or sterilized longbones) and a dog bed or collapsible crate are musts for housetraining. Three additional tools are required:

1. specific lures (training treats and toys) to predict and prompt specific desired behaviors;
2. rewards (praise, affection, training treats and toys) to reinforce for the dog what a lot of fun it all is; and
3. knowledge—how to convert the dog's favorite activities and games (potential distractions to training) into "life-rewards," which may be employed to facilitate training.

Punishment training teaches your pet not to misbehave when you are present, but frequently leads her to get into trouble once you've gone away.

The most powerful of these is knowledge. Education is the key! Watch training classes, participate in training classes, watch videos, read books, enjoy play-training with your dog and then your dog will say "Please," and your dog will say "Thank you!"

Housetraining

If dogs were left to their own devices, certainly they would chew, dig and bark for entertainment and then no doubt highlight a few areas of their living space with sprinkles of urine, in much the same way we decorate by hanging pictures. Consequently, when we ask a dog to live with us, we must teach her *where* she may dig, *where* she may perform her toilet duties, *what* she may chew and *when* she may bark. After all, when left at home alone for many hours, we cannot expect the dog to amuse herself by completing crosswords or watching TV!

Also, it would be decidedly unfair to keep the house rules a secret from the dog, and then get angry and punish the poor critter for inevitably transgressing rules she did not even know existed. Remember: Without adequate education and guidance, the dog will be forced to establish her own rules—doggy rules—and most probably will be at odds with the owner's view of domestic living.

Since most problems develop during the first few days the dog is at home, prospective dog owners must be certain they are quite clear about the principles of housetraining *before* they get a dog. Early misbehaviors quickly become established as the *status quo*—becoming firmly entrenched as hard-to-break bad habits, which set the precedent for years to come. Make sure to teach your dog good habits right from the start. Good habits are just as hard to break as bad ones!

Ideally, when a new dog comes home, try to arrange for someone to be present as much as possible during the first few days (for adult dogs) or weeks for puppies. With only a little forethought, it is surprisingly easy to find a puppy sitter, such as a retired person, who would be willing to eat from your refrigerator and watch your television while keeping an eye on the newcomer to encourage the dog to play with chew toys and to ensure she goes outside on a regular basis.

Potty Training

Follow these steps to teach the dog where she should relieve herself:

1. never let her make a single mistake;

2. let her know where you want her to go; and

3. handsomely reward her for doing so: "GOOOOOOOD DOG!!!" liver treat, liver treat, liver treat!

Preventing Mistakes

A single mistake is a training disaster, since it heralds many more in future weeks. And each time the dog soils the house, this further reinforces the dog's unfortunate preference for an indoor, carpeted toilet. Do not let an unhousetrained dog have full run of the house.

When you are away from home, or cannot pay full attention, confine the dog to an area where elimination is appropriate, such as an outdoor run or, better still, a small, comfortable indoor kennel with access to an outdoor run. When confined in this manner, most dogs will naturally housetrain themselves.

If that's not possible, confine the dog to an area, such as a utility room, kitchen, basement or garage, where elimination may not be desired in the long run but as an interim measure it is certainly preferable to doing it all around the house. Use newspaper to cover the floor of the dog's day room. The newspaper may be used to soak up the urine and to wrap up and dispose of the feces. Once your dog develops a preferred spot for eliminating, it is only necessary to cover that part of the floor with newspaper. The smaller papered area may then be moved (only a little each day) towards the door to the outside. Thus the dog will develop the tendency to go to the door when she needs to relieve herself.

Never confine an unhousetrained dog to a crate for long periods. Doing so would force the dog to soil the crate and ruin its usefulness as an aid for housetraining (see the following discussion).

Teaching Where

In order to teach your dog where you would like her to do her business, you have to be there to direct the proceedings—an obvious, yet often neglected, fact of life. In order to be there to teach the dog where to go, you need to know *when* she needs to go. Indeed, the success of housetraining depends on the owner's ability to predict these

When you must leave your puppy by herself during the day, paper-training is a good way to begin the house-breaking process.

times. Certainly, a regular feeding schedule will facilitate prediction somewhat, but there is nothing like "loading the deck" and influencing the timing of the outcome yourself!

Whenever you are at home, make sure the dog is under constant supervision and/or confined to a small area. If already well trained, simply instruct the dog to lie down in her bed or basket. Alternatively, confine the dog to a crate (doggy den) or tie-down (a short, 18-inch lead that can be clipped to an eye hook in the baseboard near her bed). Short-term close confinement strongly inhibits urination and defecation, since the dog does not want to soil her sleeping area. Thus, when you release the puppydog each hour, she will definitely need to urinate immediately and defecate every third or fourth hour. Keep the dog confined to her doggy den and take her to her intended toilet area each hour, every hour and on the hour. When taking your dog outside, instruct her to sit quietly before opening the door—she will soon learn to sit by the door when she needs to go out!

Teaching Why

Being able to predict when the dog needs to go enables the owner to be on the spot to praise and reward the dog. Each hour, hurry the dog to the intended toilet area in the yard, issue the appropriate instruction ("Go pee!" or "Go poop!"), then give the dog three to four minutes to produce. Praise and offer a couple of training treats when successful. The treats are important because many people fail to praise their dogs with feeling . . . and housetraining is hardly the time for understatement. So either loosen up and enthusiastically praise that dog: "Wuzzzer-wuzzer-wuzzer, hoooser good wuffer den? Hoooo went pee for Daddy?" Or say "Good dog!" as best you can and offer the treats for effect.

Following elimination is an ideal time for a spot of play-training in the yard or house. Also, an empty dog may be allowed greater freedom around the house for the next half hour or so, just as long as you keep an eye out to make sure she does not get into other kinds of mischief. If you are preoccupied and cannot pay full attention, confine the dog to her doggy den once more to enjoy a peaceful snooze or to play with her many chew toys.

If your dog does not eliminate within the allotted time outside—no biggie! Back to her doggy den, and then try again after another hour.

As I own large dogs, I always feel more relaxed walking an empty dog, knowing that I will not need to finish our stroll weighted down with bags of feces!

Beware of falling into the trap of walking the dog to get her to eliminate. The good ol' dog walk is such an enormous highlight in the dog's life that it represents the single biggest potential reward in domestic dogdom. However, when in a hurry, or during inclement weather, many owners abruptly terminate the walk the moment the dog has done her business. This, in effect, severely punishes the dog for doing the right thing, in the right place at the right time. Consequently, many dogs become strongly inhibited from eliminating outdoors because they know it will signal an abrupt end to an otherwise thoroughly enjoyable walk.

Instead, instruct the dog to relieve herself in the yard prior to going for a walk. If you follow the above instructions, most dogs soon learn to eliminate on cue. As soon as the dog eliminates, praise (and offer a treat or two)—"Good dog! Let's go walkies!" Use the walk as a reward for eliminating in the yard. If the dog does not go, put her back in her doggy den and think about a walk later on. You will find with a "No feces—no walk" policy, your dog will become one of the fastest defecators in the business.

If you do not have a backyard, instruct the dog to eliminate right outside your front door prior to the walk. Not only will this facilitate clean up and disposal of the feces in your own trash can but, also, the walk may again be used as a colossal reward.

Chewing and Barking

Short-term close confinement also teaches the dog that occasional quiet moments are a reality of domestic living. Your puppydog is extremely impressionable during her first few weeks at home. Regular confinement at this time soon exerts a calming influence over the dog's personality. Remember, once the dog is housetrained and calmer, there will be a whole lifetime ahead for the dog to enjoy full run of the house and garden. On the other hand, by letting the newcomer have unrestricted access to the entire household and allowing her to run willy-nilly, she will most certainly develop a bunch of behavior problems in short order, no doubt necessitating confinement later in life. It would not be fair to remedially restrain and confine a dog you have trained, through neglect, to run free.

When confining the dog, make sure she always has an impressive array of suitable chew toys. Kongs and sterilized longbones (both readily available from pet stores) make the best chew toys, since they are hollow and may be stuffed with treats to heighten the dog's interest. For example, by stuffing the little hole at the top of a Kong with a small piece of freeze-dried liver, the dog will not want to leave it alone.

Remember, treats do not have to be junk food and they certainly should not represent extra calories. Rather, treats should be part of each dog's regular daily diet: Some food may be served in the dog's bowl for breakfast and dinner, some food may be used as training treats, and some food may be used for stuffing chew toys. I regularly stuff my dogs' many Kongs with different shaped biscuits and kibble. The kibble seems to fall out fairly easily, as do the oval-shaped biscuits, thus rewarding the dog instantaneously for checking out the chew toys. The bone-shaped biscuits fall out after a while, rewarding the dog for worrying at the chew toy. But the triangular biscuits never come out. They remain inside the Kong as lures, maintaining the dog's fascination with her chew toy. To further focus the dog's interest, I always make sure to flavor the triangular biscuits by rubbing them with a little cheese or freeze-dried liver.

If stuffed chew toys are reserved especially for times the dog is confined, the puppydog will soon learn to enjoy quiet moments in her doggy den and she will quickly develop a chew-toy habit—a good habit! This is a simple autoshaping process; all the owner has to do is set up the situation and the dog all but trains herself—easy and effective. Even when the dog is given run of the house, her first inclination will be to indulge her rewarding chew-toy habit rather than destroy less-attractive household articles, such as curtains, carpets, chairs and compact disks. Similarly, a chew-toy chewer will be less inclined to scratch and chew herself excessively. Also, if the dog busies herself as a recreational chewer, she will be less inclined to develop into a recreational barker or digger when left at home alone.

Stuff a number of chew toys whenever the dog is left confined and remove the extra-special-tasting treats when you return. Your dog will now amuse herself with her chew toys before falling asleep and then resume playing with her chew toys when she expects you to return. Since most owner-absent misbehavior happens right after you leave and right before your expected return, your puppydog will now be conveniently preoccupied with her chew toys at these times.

Come and Sit

Most puppies will happily approach virtually anyone, whether called or not; that is, until they collide with adolescence and develop other more important doggy interests, such as sniffing a multiplicity of exquisite odors on the grass. Your mission, Mr./Ms. Owner, is to teach and reward the pup for coming reliably, willingly and happily when called—and you have just three months to get it done. Unless adequately reinforced, your puppy's tendency to approach people will self-destruct by adolescence.

Call your dog ("Fido, come!"), open your arms (and maybe squat down) as a welcoming signal, waggle a treat or toy as a lure and reward the puppydog when she comes running. Do not wait to praise the dog until she reaches you—she may come 95 percent of the way and then run off after some distraction. Instead, praise the dog's first step towards you and continue praising enthusiastically for every step she takes in your direction.

When the rapidly approaching puppy dog is three lengths away from impact, instruct her to sit ("Fido, sit!") and hold the lure in front of you in an outstretched hand to prevent her from hitting you mid-chest and knocking you flat on your back! As Fido decelerates to nose the lure, move the treat upwards and backwards just over her muzzle with an upwards motion of your extended arm (palm-upwards). As the dog looks up to follow the lure, she will sit down (if she jumps up, you are holding the lure too high). Praise the dog for sitting. Move backwards and call her again. Repeat this many times over, always praising when Fido comes and sits; on occasion, reward her.

For the first couple of trials, use a training treat both as a lure to entice the dog to come and sit and as a reward for doing so. Thereafter, try to use different items as lures and rewards. For example, lure the dog with a Kong or Frisbee but reward her with a food treat. Or lure the dog with a food treat but pat her and throw a tennis ball as a reward. After just a few repetitions, dispense with the lures and rewards; the dog will begin to respond willingly to your verbal requests and hand signals just for the prospect of praise from your heart and affection from your hands.

Instruct every family member, friend and visitor how to get the dog to come and sit. Invite people over for a series of pooch parties; do not keep the pup a secret—let other people enjoy this puppy, and let the pup enjoy other people. Puppydog parties are not only fun, they easily attract a lot of people to help you train your dog. Unless you teach your dog how to meet people, that

To teach come, call your dog, open your arms as a welcoming signal, wave a toy or a treat and praise for every step in your direction.

is, to sit for greetings, no doubt the dog will resort to jumping up. Then you and the visitors will get annoyed, and the dog will be punished. This is not fair. Send out those invitations for puppy parties and teach your dog to be mannerly and socially acceptable.

Even though your dog quickly masters obedient recalls in the house, her reliability may falter when playing in the backyard or local park. Ironically, it is the owner who has unintentionally trained the dog not to respond in these instances. By allowing the dog to play and run around and otherwise have a good time, but then to call the dog to put her on leash to take her home, the dog quickly learns playing is fun but training is a drag. Thus, playing in the park becomes a severe distraction, which works against training. Bad news!

Instead, whether playing with the dog off leash or on leash, request her to come at frequent intervals—say, every minute or so. On most occasions, praise and pet the dog for a few seconds while she is sitting, then tell her to go play again. For especially fast recalls, offer a couple of training treats and take the time to praise and pet the dog enthusiastically before releasing her. The dog will learn that coming when called is not necessarily the end of the play session, and neither is it the end of the world; rather, it signals an enjoyable, quality time-out with the owner before resuming play once more. In fact, playing in the park now becomes a very effective life-reward, which works to facilitate training by reinforcing each obedient and timely recall. Good news!

Sit, Down, Stand and Rollover

Teaching the dog a variety of body positions is easy for owner and dog, impressive for spectators and extremely useful for all. Using lure-reward techniques, it is possible to train several positions at once to verbal commands or hand signals (which impress the socks off onlookers).

Sit and down—the two control commands—prevent or resolve nearly a hundred behavior problems. For example, if the dog happily and obediently sits or lies down when requested, she cannot jump on visitors, dash out the front door, run around and chase her tail, pester other dogs, harass cats or annoy family, friends or strangers. Additionally, “Sit” or “Down” are the best emergency commands for off-leash control.

It is easier to teach and maintain a reliable sit than maintain a reliable recall. Sit is the purest and simplest of commands—either the dog is sitting or she is not. If there is any change of circumstances or potential danger in the park, for example, simply instruct the dog to sit. If she sits, you have a number of options: Allow the dog to resume playing when she is safe, walk up and put the dog on leash or call the dog. The dog will be much more likely to come when called if she has already acknowledged her compliance by sitting. If the dog does not sit in the park—train her to!

Stand and rollover-stay are the two positions for examining the dog. Your veterinarian will love you to distraction if you take a little time to teach the dog to stand still and roll over and play possum. Also, your vet bills will be smaller because it will take the veterinarian less time to examine your dog. The rollover-stay is an especially useful command and is really just a variation of the down-stay: Whereas the dog lies prone in the traditional down, she lies supine in the rollover-stay.

As with teaching come and sit, the training techniques to teach the dog to assume all other body positions on cue are user-friendly and dog-friendly. Simply give the appropriate request, lure the dog into the desired body position using a training treat or toy and then praise (and maybe reward) the dog as soon as she complies. Try not to touch the dog to get her to respond. If you teach the dog by guiding her into position, the dog will quickly learn that rump-pressure means sit, for example, but as yet you still have no control over your dog if she is just 6 feet away. It will still be necessary to teach the dog to sit on request. So do not make training a time-consuming two-step process; instead, teach the dog to sit to a verbal request or hand signal from the outset. Once the dog sits willingly when requested, by all means use your hands to pet the dog when she does so.

To teach down when the dog is already sitting, say “Fido, down!”, hold the lure in one hand (palm down) and lower that hand to the floor between the dog’s forepaws. As the dog lowers her head to follow the lure, slowly move the lure away from the dog just a fraction (in front of her paws). The dog will lie down as she stretches her nose forward to follow the lure. Praise the dog when she does so. If the dog stands up, you pulled the lure away too far and too quickly.

When teaching the dog to lie down from the standing position, say "Down" and lower the lure to the floor as before. Once the dog has lowered her forequarters and assumed a play bow, gently and slowly move the lure towards the dog between her forelegs. Praise the dog as soon as her rear end plops down.

After just a couple of trials it will be possible to alternate sits and downs and have the dog energetically perform doggy push-ups. Praise the dog a lot, and after half a dozen or so push-ups reward the dog with a training treat or toy. You will notice the more energetically you move your arm—upwards (palm up) to get the dog to sit, and downwards (palm down) to get the dog to lie down—the more energetically the dog responds to your requests. Now try training the dog in silence and you will notice she has also learned to respond to hand signals. Yeah! Not too shabby for the first session.

To teach stand from the sitting position, say "Fido, stand," slowly move the lure half a dog-length away from the dog's nose, keeping it at nose level, and praise the dog as she stands to follow the lure. As soon as the dog stands, lower the lure to just beneath the dog's chin to entice her to look down; otherwise she will stand and then sit immediately. To prompt the dog to stand from the down position, move the lure half a dog-length upwards and away from the dog, holding the lure at standing nose height from the floor.

Teaching rollover is best started from the down position, with the dog lying on one side, or at least with both hind legs stretched out on the same side. Say "Fido, bang!" and move the lure backwards and alongside the dog's muzzle to her elbow (on the side of her outstretched hind legs). Once the dog looks to the side and backwards, very slowly move the lure upwards to the dog's shoulder and backbone. Tickling the dog in the goolies (groin area) often invokes a reflex-raising of the hind leg as an appeasement gesture, which facilitates the tendency to roll over. If you move the lure too quickly and the dog jumps into the standing position, have patience

Using a food lure to teach sit, down and stand.
1) "Phoenix, sit."
2) Hand palm upwards, move lure up and back over dog's muzzle.
3) "Good sit, Phoenix!"

4) "Phoenix, down." 5) Hand palm downwards, move lure down to lie between dog's forepaws.
6) "Phoenix, off. Good down, Phoenix!"

7) "Phoenix, sit!"
8) Palm upwards, move lure up and back, keeping it close to dog's muzzle.
9) "Good sit, Phoenix!"

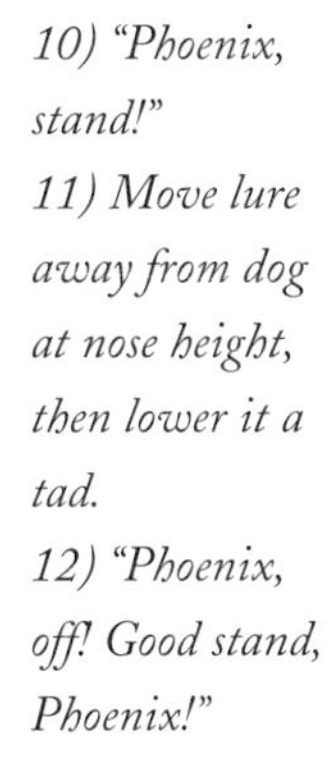

10) "Phoenix, stand!"
11) Move lure away from dog at nose height, then lower it a tad.
12) "Phoenix, off! Good stand, Phoenix!"

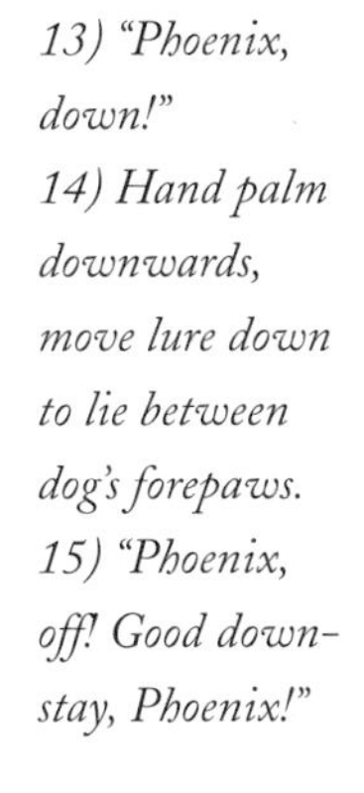

13) "Phoenix, down!"
14) Hand palm downwards, move lure down to lie between dog's forepaws.
15) "Phoenix, off! Good down-stay, Phoenix!"

16) "Phoenix, stand!"
17) Move lure away from dog's muzzle up to nose height.
18) "Phoenix, off! Good stand-stay, Phoenix. Now we'll make the vet and groomer happy!"

and start again. As soon as the dog rolls onto her back, keep the lure stationary and mesmerize the dog with a relaxing tummy rub.

To teach rollover-stay when the dog is standing or moving, say "Fido, bang!" and give the appropriate hand signal (with index finger pointed and thumb cocked in true Sam Spade fashion), then in one fluid movement lure her to first lie down and then rollover-stay as above.

Teaching the dog to stay in each of the above four positions becomes a piece of cake after first teaching the dog not to worry at the toy or treat training lure. This is best accomplished by hand feeding dinner kibble. Hold a piece of kibble firmly in your hand and softly instruct "Off!" Ignore any licking and slobbering for however long the dog worries at the treat, but say "Take it!" and offer the kibble *the instant* the dog breaks contact with her muzzle. Repeat this a few times, and then up the ante and insist the dog remove her muzzle for one whole second before offering the kibble. Then progressively refine your criteria and have the dog not touch your hand (or treat) for longer and longer periods on each trial, such as for two seconds, four seconds, then six, ten, fifteen, twenty, thirty seconds and so on.

The dog soon learns: (1) worrying at the treat never gets results, whereas (2) noncontact is often rewarded after a variable time lapse.

Teaching "Off!" has many useful applications in its own right. Additionally, instructing the dog not to touch a training lure often produces spontaneous and magical stays. Request the dog to stand-stay, for example, and not to touch the lure. At first set your sights on a short two-second stay before rewarding the dog. (Remember, every long journey begins with a single step.) However, on subsequent trials, gradually and progressively increase the length of stay required to receive a reward. In no time at all your dog will stand calmly for a minute or so.

Relevancy Training

Once you have taught the dog what you expect her to do when requested to come, sit, lie down, stand, rollover and stay, the time is right to teach the dog why she should comply with your wishes. The secret is to have many (many) extremely short training interludes (two to five seconds each) at numerous (numerous) times during the course of the dog's day. Especially work with the dog immediately before the dog's good times and during the dog's good times. For example, ask your dog to sit and/or lie down each time before opening doors, serving meals, offering treats and tummy rubs; ask the dog to perform a few controlled doggy push-ups before letting her off leash or throwing a tennis ball; and perhaps request the dog to sit-down-sit-stand-down-stand-rollover before inviting her to cuddle on the couch.

Similarly, request the dog to sit many times during play or on walks, and in no time at all the dog will be only too pleased to follow your instructions because she has learned that a compliant response heralds all sorts of goodies. Basically all you are trying to teach the dog is how to say please: "Please throw the tennis ball. Please may I snuggle on the couch."

Remember, it is important to keep training interludes short and to have many short sessions each and every day. The shortest (and most useful) session comprises asking the dog to sit and then go play during a play session. When trained this way, your dog will soon associate training with good times. In fact, the dog may be unable to distinguish between training and good times and, indeed, there should be no distinction. The warped concept that training involves forcing the dog to comply and/or dominating her will is totally at odds with the picture of a truly well-trained dog. In reality, enjoying a game of training with a dog is no different from enjoying a game of backgammon or tennis with a friend; and walking with a dog should be no different from strolling with a spouse, or with buddies on the golf course.

Walk by Your Side

Many people attempt to teach a dog to heel by putting her on a leash and physically correcting the dog when she makes mistakes. There are a number of things seriously wrong with this approach, the first being that most people do not want precision heeling; rather, they simply want the dog to follow or walk by their side. Second, when physically restrained during "training," even though the dog may grudgingly mope by your side when "handcuffed" on leash, let's see what happens when she is off leash. History! The dog is in the next county because she never enjoyed walking with you on leash and you have no control over her off leash. So let's just teach the dog off leash from the outset to want to walk with us. Third, if the dog has not been trained to heel, it is a trifle hasty to think about punishing the poor dog for making mistakes and breaking heeling rules she didn't even know existed. This is simply not fair! Surely, if the dog had been adequately taught how to heel, she would seldom make mistakes and hence there would be no need to correct the dog. Remember, each mistake and each correction (punishment) advertise the trainer's inadequacy, not the dog's. The dog is not stubborn, she is not stupid and she is not bad. Even if she were, she would still require training, so let's train her properly.

Let's teach the dog to enjoy following us and to want to walk by our side off leash. Then it will be easier to teach high-precision off-leash heeling patterns if desired. Before going on outdoor walks, it is necessary to teach the dog not to pull. Then it becomes easy to teach on-leash walking and heeling because the dog already wants to walk with you, she is familiar with the desired walking and heeling positions and she knows not to pull.

Following

Start by training your dog to follow you. Many puppies will follow if you simply walk away from them and maybe click your fingers or chuckle. Adult dogs may require additional enticement to stimulate them to follow, such as a training lure or, at the very least, a lively trainer. To teach the dog to follow: (1) keep walking and (2) walk away from the dog. If the dog attempts to lead or lag, change pace; slow down if the dog forges too far ahead, but speed up if she lags too far behind. Say "Steady!" or "Easy!" each time before you slow down and "Quickly!" or "Hustle!" each time before you speed up, and the dog will learn to change pace on cue. If the dog lags or leads too far, or if she wanders right or left, simply walk quickly in the opposite direction and maybe even run away from the dog and hide.

Practicing is a lot of fun; you can set up a course in your home, yard or park to do this. Indoors, entice the dog to follow upstairs, into a bedroom, into the bathroom, downstairs, around the living room couch, zigzagging between dining room chairs and into the kitchen for dinner. Outdoors, get the dog to follow around park benches, trees, shrubs and along walkways and lines in the grass. (For safety outdoors, it is advisable to attach a long line on the dog, but never exert corrective tension on the line.)

Remember, following has a lot to do with attitude—your attitude! Most probably your dog will not want to follow Mr. Grumpy Troll with the personality of wilted lettuce. Lighten up—walk with a jaunty step, whistle a happy tune, sing, skip and tell jokes to your dog and she will be right there by your side.

By Your Side

It is smart to train the dog to walk close on one side or the other—either side will do, your choice. When walking, jogging or cycling, it is generally bad news to have the dog suddenly cut in front of you. In fact, I train my dogs to walk "By my side" and "Other side"—both very useful instructions. It is possible to position the dog fairly accurately by looking to the appropriate side and clicking your fingers or slapping your thigh on that side. A precise positioning may be attained by holding a training lure, such as a chew toy, tennis ball, or food treat. Stop and stand still several times throughout the walk, just as you would when window shopping or meeting a friend. Use the lure to make sure the dog slows down and stays close whenever you stop.

When teaching the dog to heel, we generally want her to sit in heel position when we stop. Teach heel position at the standstill and the dog will learn that the default heel position is sitting by your side (left or right—your choice, unless you wish to compete in obedience trials, in which case the dog must heel on the left).

Several times a day, stand up and call your dog to come and sit in heel position—"Fido, heel!" For example, instruct the dog to come to heel each time there are commercials on TV, or each time you turn a page of a novel, and the dog will get it in a single evening.

Practice straight-line heeling and turns separately. With the dog sitting at heel, teach her to turn in place. After each quarter-turn, half-turn or full turn in place, lure the dog to sit at heel. Now it's time for short straight-line heeling sequences, no more than a few steps at a time. Always think of heeling in terms of sit-heel-sit sequences—start and end with the dog in position and do your best to keep her there when moving. Progressively increase the number of steps in each sequence. When the dog remains close for 20 yards of straight-line heeling, it is time to add a few turns and then sign up for a happy-heeling obedience class to get some advice from the experts.

It's not hard to convince a young puppy to walk on leash—her natural instinct is to follow you.

No Pulling on Leash

You can start teaching your dog not to pull on leash anywhere—in front of the television or outdoors—but regardless of location, you must not take a single step with tension in the leash. For a reason known only to dogs, even just a couple of paces of pulling on leash is intrinsically motivating and diabolically rewarding. Instead, attach the leash to the dog's collar, grasp the other end firmly with both hands held close to your chest, and stand still—do not budge an inch. Have somebody watch you with a stopwatch to time your progress, or else you will never believe this will work and so you will not even try the exercise, and your shoulder and the dog's neck will be traumatized for years to come.

Stand still and wait for the dog to stop pulling, and to sit and/or lie down. All dogs stop pulling and sit eventually. Most take only a couple of minutes; the all-time record is 22 ½ minutes. Time how long it takes. Gently praise the dog when she stops pulling, and as soon as she sits, enthusiastically praise the dog and take just one step forwards, then immediately stand still. This single step usually demonstrates the ballistic reinforcing nature of pulling on leash; most dogs explode to the end of the leash, so be prepared for the strain. Stand firm and wait for the dog to sit again. Repeat this half a dozen times and you will probably notice a progressive reduction in the force of the dog's one-step explosions and a radical reduction in the time it takes for the dog to sit each time.

As the dog learns "Sit we go" and "Pull we stop," she will begin to walk forward calmly with each single step and automatically sit when you stop. Now try two steps before you stop. Wooooooo! Scary! When the dog has mastered two steps at a time, try for three. After each success, progressively increase the number of steps in the sequence: try four steps and then six, eight, ten and twenty steps before stopping. Congratulations! You are now walking the dog on leash.

Whenever walking with the dog (off leash or on leash), make sure you stop periodically to practice a few position commands and stays before instructing the dog to "Walk on!"

Integrating training into a walk offers 200 separate opportunities to use the continuance of the walk as a reward to reinforce the dog's education.

A well-trained German Shepherd will walk easily and calmly on leash by your side.

Further Reading and Resources

Books

About German Shepherd Dogs

Strickland, Winnifred Gibson and James A. Moses. *The German Shepherd Today.* New York: Howell Book House, 1998.

About Health Care

American Kennel Club. *American Kennel Club Dog Care and Training.* New York: Howell Book House, 1991.

Carlson, Delbert, DVM, and James Giffen, MD. *Dog Owner's Home Veterinary Handbook.* New York: Howell Book House, 1992.

DeBitetto, James, DVM, and Sarah Hodgson. *You & Your Puppy.* New York: Howell Book House, 1995.

Schwartz, Stefanie, DVM. *First Aid for Dogs: An Owner's Guide to a Happy Healthy Pet.* New York: Howell Book House, 1998.

About Training

Ammen, Amy. *Training in No Time.* New York: Howell Book House, 1995.

Dunbar, Ian, PhD, MRCVS. *Dr. Dunbar's Good Little Book.* James & Kenneth Publishers, 2140 Shattuck Ave. #2406, Berkeley, CA 94704. (510) 658-8588. Order from publisher.

———Dunbar, Ian, PhD, MRCVS. *How to Teach a New Dog Old Tricks.* James & Kenneth Publishers. Order from publisher; see address above.

Ryan, Terry. *The Toolbox for Remodeling Your Problem Dog.* New York: Howell Book House, 1998.

About Activities

American Rescue Dog Association. *Search and Rescue Dogs.* New York: Howell Book House, 1991.

Barwig, Susan and Stewart Hilliard. *Schutzhund.* New York: Howell Book House, 1991.

Davis, Kathy Diamond. *Therapy Dogs.* New York: Howell Book House, 1992.

Holland, Vergil S. *Herding Dogs.* New York: Howell Book House, 1994.

MAGAZINES

The AKC GAZETTE, The Official Journal for the Sport of Purebred Dogs
American Kennel Club
51 Madison Ave.
New York, NY 10010

Dog Fancy
Fancy Publications
3 Burroughs
Irvine, CA 92718

Dog World

Maclean Hunter Publishing Corp.
29 N. Wacker Dr.
Chicago, IL 60606

German Shepherd Dog Review
30 Far View Rd.
Chalfont, PA 18914

German Shepherd Dog Quarterly
Hoflin Publishing, Inc.
4401 Zephyr St.
Wheat Ridge, CO 80033–3299

MORE INFORMATION ON GERMAN SHEPHERD DOGS

National Breed Club

German Shepherd Dog Club of America, Inc.
Blanche Beisswenger, Corresponding Secretary
17 West Ivy Lane
Englewood, NJ 07631

The club can send you information on the breed itself as well as the names and locations of local dog clubs or German Shepherd Dog clubs in your area. It can also provide information on obedience and herding clubs and other ways to get active with your German Shepherd Dog. Inquire about membership.

Resources

The American Kennel Club

The American Kennel Club, devoted to the advancement of purebred dogs, is the oldest and largest registry organization in this country. Every breed recognized by the AKC has a national (parent) club. National clubs are a great source of information on your breed. The affiliated clubs hold AKC events and use AKC rules to hold performance events, dog shows, educational programs, health clinics and training classes. The AKC staff is divided between offices in New York City and Raleigh, North Carolina. All registration functions are done in North Carolina.

For registration and performance events information, contact:

THE AMERICAN KENNEL CLUB
5580 Centerview Drive, Suite 200
Raleigh, NC 27606
Phone: (919) 233-9767
Fax: (919) 233-3627
E-mail: info@akc.org

For obedience information, contact:

THE AMERICAN KENNEL CLUB
51 Madison Ave.
New York, NY 10010
Phone: (212) 696-8276
Fax: (212) 696-8272
E-mail: www.akc.org

For information on AKC Companion Animal Recovery, contact:

Phone: (800) 252-7894
Fax: (919) 233-1290
E-mail: found@akc.org

TRAINERS

ASSOCIATION OF PET DOG TRAINERS
P.O. Box 385
Davis, CA 95617
(800) PET-DOGS